AF530279

# Copper Oxide & Silver Phosphate Nanoparticles and their bio-medical and environmental applications

Palpandi. K

SPI PUBLICATIONS

This book has been published with all reasonable efforts taken to make the material error-free after the consent of the author. No part of this book shall be used, reproduced in any manner whatsoever without written permission from the author, except in the case of brief quotations embodied in critical articles and reviews.

The Author of this book is solely responsible and liable for its content including but not limited to the views, representations, descriptions, statements, information, opinions and references ["Content"]. The Content of this book shall not constitute or be construed or deemed to reflect the opinion or expression of the Publisher or Editor. Neither the Publisher nor Editor endorse or approve the Content of this book or guarantee the reliability, accuracy or completeness of the Content published herein and do not make any representations or warranties of any kind, express or implied, including but not limited to the implied warranties of merchantability, fitness for a particular purpose. The Publisher and Editor shall not be liable whatsoever for any errors, omissions, whether such errors or omissions result from negligence, accident, or any other cause or claims for loss or damages of any kind, including without limitation, indirect or consequential loss or damage arising out of use, inability to use, or about the reliability, accuracy or sufficiency of the information contained in this book.

Published by **SPI Publications**, www.spipublications.in

**SPI**, the **SPI logo**, and **Split Poetry India** are trademarks of **SPI Publications**, or its affiliates.

**ISBN-13: 978-93-49860-95-7**

**First Edition 2025**

**SPI Publications**

**Corporate & Editorial Office**
**117/2, Sector 37, Khandsa Road,**
**Gurgaon, Haryana 122 001**
**Phone: +91 98355 52940**
**Email: contact@spipublications.in**
**Website: www.spipublications.in**

**Processed and Printed in India**

## Author details

*"Palpandi. K, is a quality control data analyst specializing in photocatalyst, graphene oxide synthesis, electrochemical sensor fabrications. He has contributed to various open-source projects and is passionate about using technology for social good."*

*ORCID ID:* 0009-0003-2698-3455

K. PALPANDI, B.Sc., M.Sc., MBA (SRHM), DCS, DTP, Diploma in Industrial Engineering

# CHAPTER-I

## Introduction of Nanotechnology

Nanotechnology is the use of very small pieces of materials by themselves or their manipulation to create new large-scale materials. At the nano-scale materials, properties are altered from that of larger scale material. The nano-scale is the size of range from approximately 1nm to 100nm. Nanotechnology is an enabling technology that allow as to develop materials with improved or totally new properties. Demonstration of nanotechnology in day-to-day life see in figure.

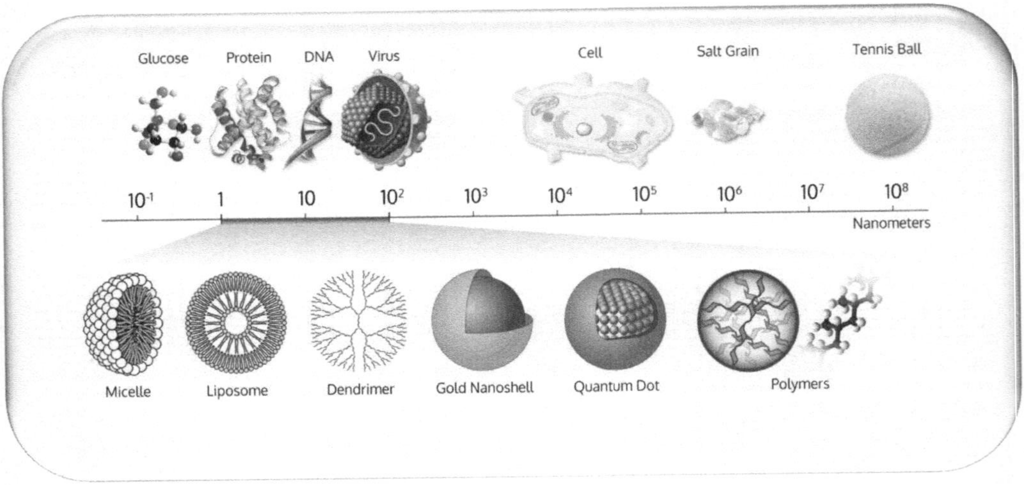


Demonstration of Nanotechnology

### *Nanomaterials*

Nanomaterials are a broadly defined set of substances that have at least one critical dimension less than 100 nanometers and possess unique optical, magnetic or electrical properties. Ultrafine particulate matter is a well-known example of nanoscale particles found in the environment. The NTP's research program focuses on manufactured nanoscale materials of current or projected commercial importance. The program includes studies to evaluate the biological disposition of nanoscale crystalline fluorescent semiconductors ("quantum dots), long-term toxicology studies of carbon-based nanoscale materials (Ex: single or multi-walled nanotubes and fullerenes).

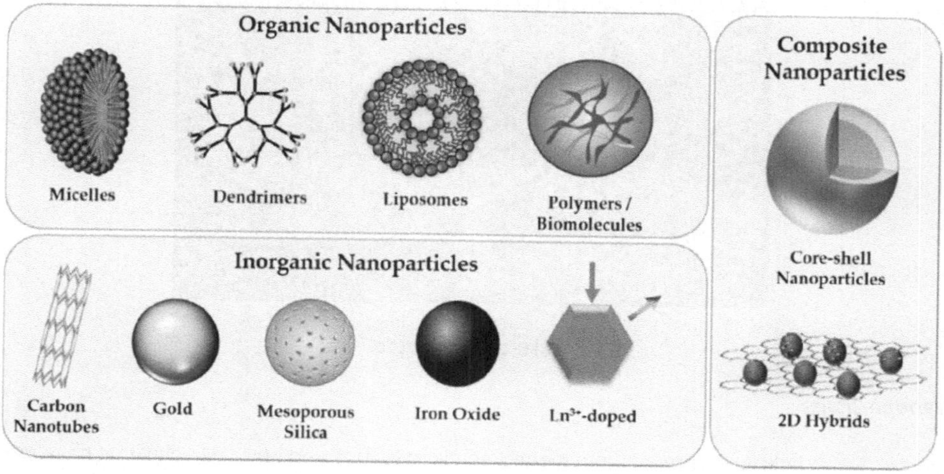


***Types of Nanomaterials***

Nanomaterials are categorized into several types based on their morphology as follows;

- Fullerenes
- Nanoparticles
- Nanotubes
- Nanowires
- Nanorods
- Nanocomposites

***Fullerenes***

Fullerenes are actually graphene sheets rolled in the form of spheres and are actually a class of allotropes of carbon. A main example of fullerene is carbon nanotubes. They are known for their mechanical strength and their good electrical conductivity. Take a look at the fullerene is in the figure.

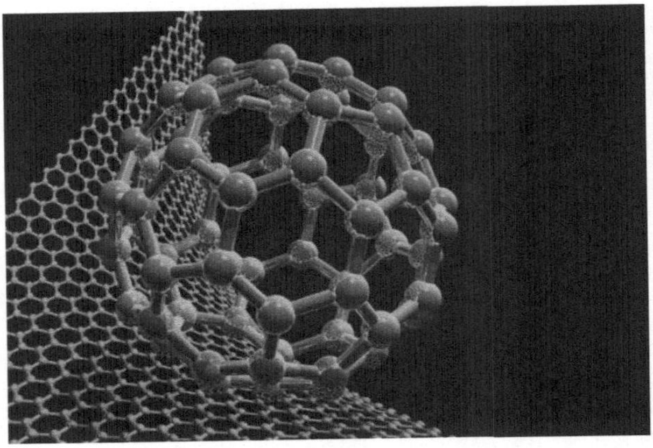

Fullerene Structure

***Nanoparticles***

Nanoparticles are made from metals, semiconductors and other particles that have great chemical, physical, electrical and magnetic properties. Nanoparticles find its main application as chemical catalysts. Nanoparticles have a size so small, that they actually lie between the bulk materials and the molecular structures. As a result, they possess some of the properties of the bulk materials as well as molecular structures.

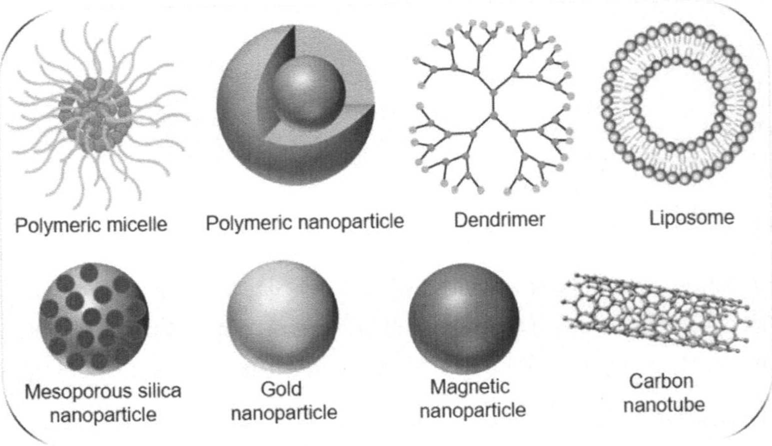

### *Nanotubes*

A Carbon Nanotube is a tube-shaped material, made of carbon, having a diameter measuring on the nanometer scale. A nanometer is one-billionth of a meter or about one ten-thousandth of the thickness of a human hair. Carbon Nanotubes have many structures, differing in length, thickness and in the type of helicity and number of layers as shown in Figure. Although they are formed from essentially the same graphite sheet, their electrical characteristics differ depending on these variations, acting either as metals or as semiconductors.

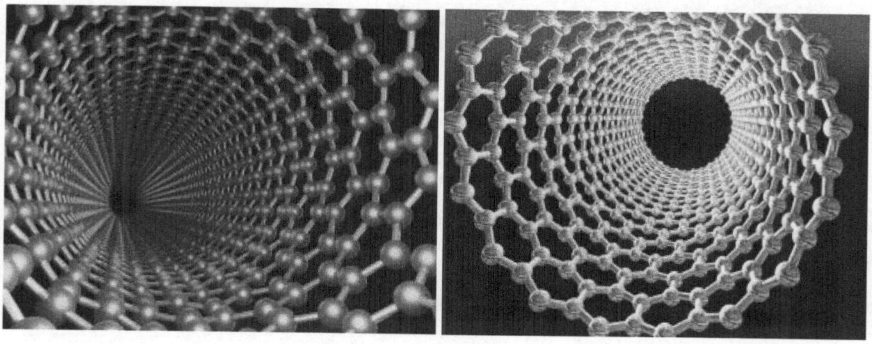

Nanotubes

### *Nanowires*

Nanowires are extremely small. Nanowires can be made from a variety of conducting and semiconducting materials like copper, silver, zinc oxide and germanium. Nanowires can also be made from carbon nanotubes. Nanowires can be defined as structures that have a thickness or diameter constrained to tens of nanometers or less and an unconstrained length.

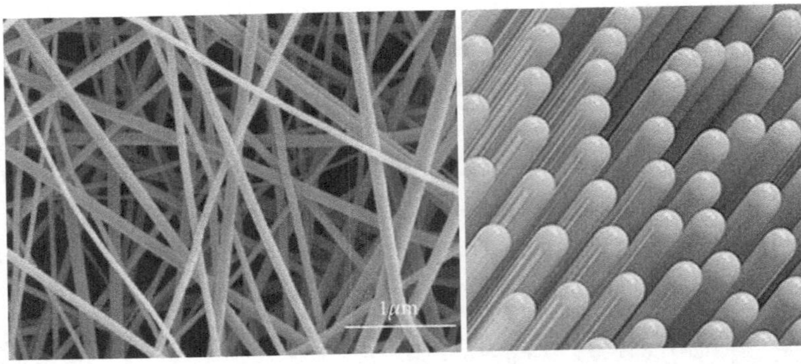


Carbon Nanowires

***Nanorods***

Nanorods is a nanosize rod which having a size measured in nanometers. Their dimensions range from 1-100nm. They may be synthesized from metals or semiconducting materials.

Nano rods

### *Nanocomposites*

Composites combine nanoparticles with other nanoparticles or with larger, bulk-type materials. Nanoparticles, such as nano-sized clays, are already being added to products ranging from auto parts to packaging materials, to enhance mechanical, thermal, barrier, and flame-retardant properties.

### *Synthesis of Nanomaterials*

There are two approaches for synthesis of nanomaterials and the fabrication of nano structures as shown in Figure. Top down approach refers to slicing or successive cutting of a bulk material to get nano-sized particle. Bottom up approach refers to the buildup of a material from the bottom: atom-by-atom, molecule-by-molecule or cluster by cluster.

Both approaches play very important role in modern industry and most likely in nano technology as well. There are advantages and disadvantages in both approaches. Attrition or Milling is a typical top down method in making nanoparticles, whereas the colloidal dispersion is a good example of bottom up approach in the synthesis of nanoparticles. The biggest problem with top down approach is the imperfection of surface structure and significant crystallographic damage to the processed patterns. These imperfections, which in turn leads to extra challenges in the device design and fabrication. But, this approach leads to the bulk production of nano material. Regardless of the defects produced by top down approach, they will continue to play an important role in the synthesis of nanostructure. Though the bottom up approach often referred in nanotechnology, it is not a newer concept. All the living beings in nature observe growth by this approach only and it has been in industrial use for over a century.

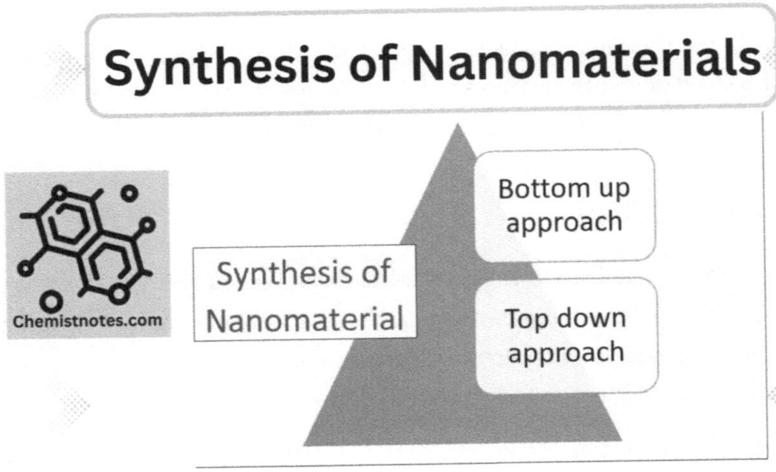


Synthesis of Nanomaterials

In the top-down approach nanoparticles are synthesized by physically slicing or by abrasion of bulk material till the desired size is achieved. This approach was practiced by Neanderthal man almost 300,000 years ago in Paleolithic period, when human race first learnt to fabricate tools. In the course of evolution human being has mastered in this art by being able to realize the structure of sub-micron level using different sophisticated techniques such as laser induced chemical etching, ball milling etc..,

The bottom-up approaches mainly involve chemical and biological methods to make nanostructures and nanoparticles. These processes involve controlled condensation of solute molecules that are formed during a chemical reaction. The restriction of the condensation or growth leads to the formation of particles of desired size and shape. However, unlike chemical synthesis of molecules with desired structure, the synthesis of nanomaterials with uniform size and shape is difficult. Thus, large-scale synthesis of nanomaterials with specific composition, uniform size and shape remains an arduous task. The control of size, shape, stability and the assembly of nanoparticles can be achieved by incorporating different capping agents, solvents and templates. Various capping agents ranging from simple ions, to polymers to biomolecules are routinely used for the capping and stabilization of nanoparticles. Figure shows various strategies for the synthesis of nanoparticles.

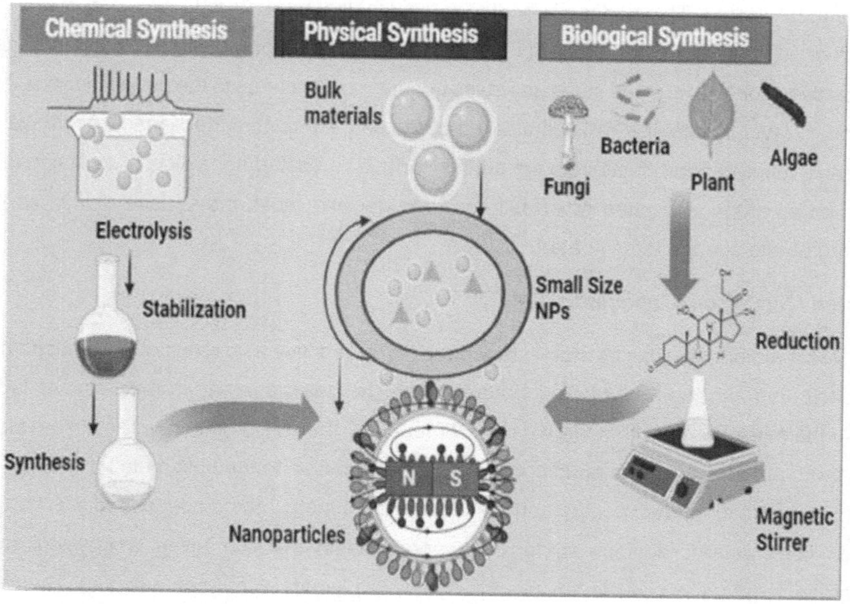


Various Approaches for Synthesis of Nanoparticles

## Physical Synthesis Methods

### *Evaporation Methods*

Physical vapor deposition (PVD), sputtering and chemical vapor deposition (CVD) are the commonly used methods to form thin films of inorganic nanomaterials. PVD involves condensation from the vapor phase. The PVD process is composed of three main steps: (a) generating a vapor phase by evaporation or sublimation of the material, (b) transporting the material from the source to the substrate, and (c) formation of the particle and/or film by nucleation and growth. Different techniques have been used to evaporate the source such as electron beam, thermal energy, sputtering, cathodic arc plasma, and pulsed laser. Si nanowire, $GeO_2$ nanowire, $Ga_2O_3$ nanowire,

ZnO nano-rod, GaO nano-belt and nanosheet, $SnO_2$ nanowire, nanoribbon, nanotube, etc., have been synthesized using PVD.

In CVD, the carrier gases containing the elements of the desired compound flow over the surface to be coated. This surface is heated to a suitable temperature to allow decomposition of the carrier gas and to allow the mobility of the deposited atoms or molecules on the surface. The CVD process consists of three steps: (a) mass transport of reactants to the growth surface through a boundary layer by diffusion, (b) chemical reactions on the growth surface, and (c) removal of the gas-phase reaction byproducts from the growth surface. In sputtering, a discharge of non-reactive ions such as argon is created which fall on the target and break the surface atoms, which are collected on the surface to be coated.

***Solvated Metal Atom Deposition (SMAD)***

Most metals vaporize as atoms, which are highly reactive as a result of the input of the heat of vaporization and the lack of steric interactions. The basic strategy in this process is to co--deposit the metal atoms with a large excess of reactant, thereby promoting reaction between the metal atom and the substrate and suppressing recombination to the bulk metal. In SMAD, a bulk metal is evaporated under vacuum and the vapors of the metal are co-condensed with vapours of organic solvents like acetone to form nanoparticles in solution using a physical method. Evaporation of metal is achieved by electrically heating a metal wire under vacuum. The resulting solution would consist only of colloids and solvent with no byproducts of gold salt. Polar protic or aprotic solvents yield generally stable colloids but those with non-polar organic solvents and water yielded large gold particles that undergo irreversible precipitation. $SiO_2$, Co-Mn and Pt-Sn alloys, metallic nanoparticles like Au etc., have been synthesized using SMAD.

***Laser Ablation***

When intense laser pulses are focused on a metal target, metal atoms present in the exposed region will be desorbed. In a Laser ablation experiment, a bulk metal is immersed in a solvent containing surfactant. During the laser irradiation, the metal atoms will vaporize and are immediately solvated by the surfactant molecules to form nanoparticles in solution. The intensity of the laser pulse and time of exposure are two parameters, which control the size of the nanoparticles formed during laser ablation. Metal nanoparticles such as gold, silver and platinum nanoparticles are prepared by this way with good control over size.

***Photolytic and Radiolytic Methods***

These methods involve the reduction of metal salts by radiolytically produced reducing agents such as solvated electrons and free radicals and the photolysis of metal complexes in the presence of some donor ligands. Radiolysis of aqueous solutions of metal ions gives solvated electrons that may directly react with the metal ions or with other dissolved materials to produce secondary radicals, which then reduce the metal ions to form nanoparticles. Alcohols are known to form radicals when they are irradiated with UV light. Radicals thus generated by this way can reduce the metal ions to form nanoparticles when UV light is irradiated on mixture of aqueous metal ions and alcohols metallic nanoparticles like gold and silver has been synthesized by this method.

**Chemical Synthesis Methods**

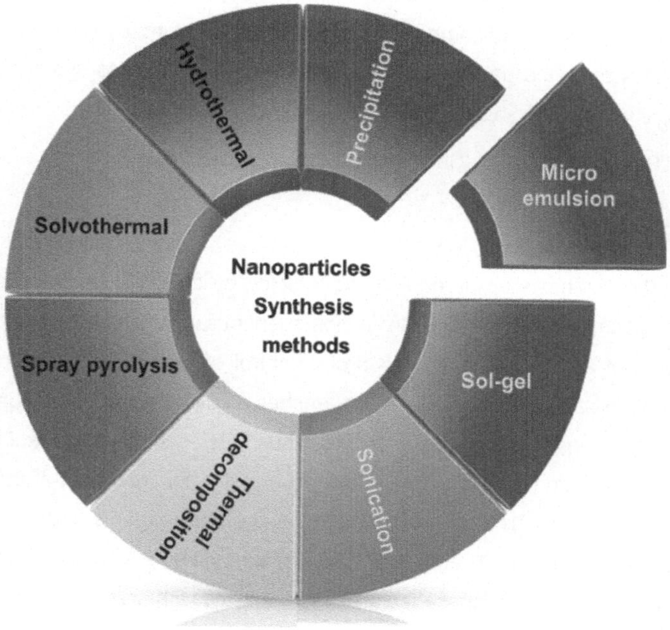

***Sol-gel Method***

The sol-gel method is based on inorganic polymerization reactions. The sol-gel process includes four different steps: hydrolysis, polycondensation, drying, and thermal decomposition. Precursors of the metal or nonmetal alkoxides hydrolyze with water or alcohols according to the hydrolysis process

$$M(OR)_x + mH_2O \rightarrow M(OR)_{x-m}(OH)_m + mROH$$

Where, if m is up to x, the reaction is total hydrolysis, followed by either a water condensation or alcohol condensation. In addition to water and alcohol, an acid or a base can also help to hydrolyze the precursor. In the case of an acid, a reaction takes place between alkoxide and the acid.

$$\text{-M-OR} + AOH \rightarrow \text{-M-O-A} + ROH$$

After the solution has been condensed to a gel, the solvent must be removed. Higher temperature calcination is needed to decompose the organic precursor. The size of the sol particles depends on the solution composition, pH, and temperature. By controlling these factors, one can tune the size of the particles. This method has been used to synthesize metal oxide nanostructures, such as $TiO_2$, $UO_2$, $TnO_2$, $ZrO_2$, $CeO_2$, SnO2, $SiO_2$, CuO, $SnO_2$, ZnO, $Al_2O_3$, $Sc_2O_3$, $ZnTiO_3$, $SrTiO_3$, $BaZrO_3$, $CaSnO_3$ and other nanostructures.

***Chemical Precipitation***

During the synthesis of inorganic nanoparticles by chemical precipitation method, the kinetics of nucleation and particle growth in homogeneous solutions can be adjusted by the controlled release of anions and cations. Careful control of precipitation kinetics can result in monodisperse nanoparticles. Once the solution reaches a critical super saturation of the species forming particles, only one burst of nuclei occurs. Thus, it is essential to control the factors that determine the precipitation process, such as the pH and the concentration of the reactants and ions. Organic molecules are used to control the release of the reagents and ions in the solution during the precipitation process. The particle size is influenced by the reactant concentration, pH, and temperature. By engineering these factors, nanoparticles with narrow size distributions, such as $Zr(OH)_4$, Ba-$TiO_3$, $YBaCu_3Oy$, CdS, HgTe, and CdTe, have been produced. Although the method of using precipitation to prepare nanoparticles is very straight forward and simple, very complicated nanostructures can also be constructed using this method such as CdS/HgS/CdS, CdS/$(HgS)_2$/CdS and HgTe/CdS quantum well systems and other core/shell structures.

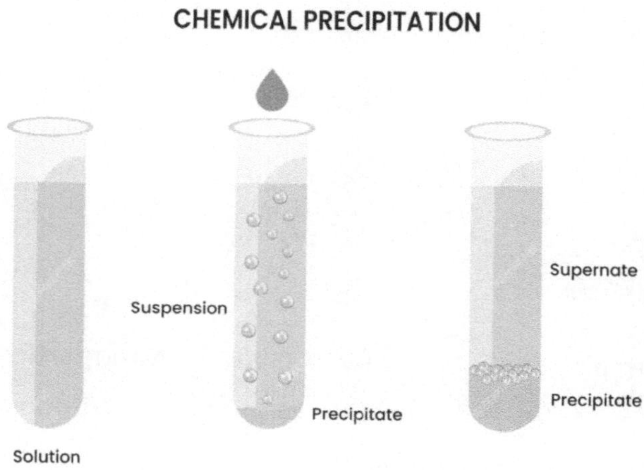


***Hydrothermal Synthesis***

Hydrothermal synthesis is a common method to synthesize zeolite/molecular sieve crystals. This method exploits the solubility of almost all inorganic substances in water at elevated temperatures and pressures and subsequent crystallization of the dissolved material from the fluid. Water at elevated temperatures plays an essential role in the precursor material transformation because the vapour pressure is much higher and the structure of water at elevated temperatures is different from that at room temperature. The properties of the reactants, including their solubility and reactivity, also change at high temperatures. The changes mentioned above provide more parameters to produce different high-quality nanoparticles and nanotubes, which are not possible at low temperatures. During the synthesis of nanocrystals, parameters such as water pressure, temperature, reaction time, and the respective precursor- product system can be tuned to maintain a high simultaneous nucleation rate and good size distribution. Different types of oxides and sulphides nanoparticles such as $TiO_2$, $LaCrO_3$, $ZrO_2$, $BaTiO_3$, $SrTiO_3$, $Y_2Si_2O_7$,

$Sb_2S_3$, CrN, α-$SnS_2$, PbS and $SnS_2$ nanotubes, $Bi_2S_3$ nanorods, and SiC nanowires have been successfully synthesized in this way. The solvent is not limited to water but also includes other polar or nonpolar solvents, such as benzene, and the process is more appropriately called solvothermal synthesis in different solvents.

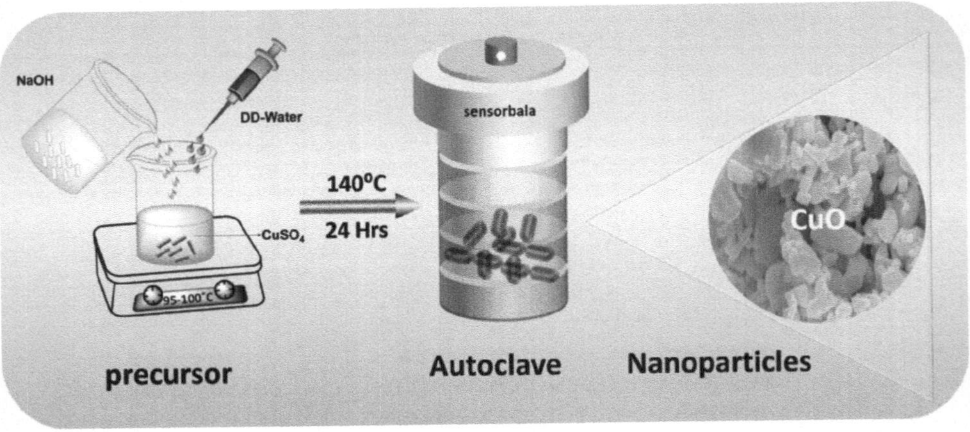


***Micelles or Micro emulsion Based Synthesis***

In this method, the synthesis of nanoparticles can be achieved by confining the reaction volume in a restricted place. When the surfactant concentration exceeds the critical micelle concentration (cmc) in water, micelles are formed as aggregates of surfactant molecules. In normal micelles, the hydrophobic hydrocarbon chains of the surfactants are oriented toward the interior of the micelle, and the hydrophilic groups of the surfactants are in contact with the surrounding aqueous medium. On the other hand, reverse micelles are formed in non-aqueous medium where the hydrophilic head groups are directed toward the core of the micelles and the hydrophobic groups are directed outward. A micro emulsion is a dispersion of fine liquid droplets of an organic solution in an aqueous solution. Such a micro emulsion system can be used for the synthesis of nanoparticles. The chemical reactions can take place either at either at the interfaces between the organic droplets and aqueous solution, when reactants are introduced separately into two immiscible solutions or inside the organic droplets when all the reactants are dissolved into the organic droplets. This method is particularly useful for the synthesis of semiconductor, oxide and metal nanoparticles such as CdSe, CdTe, CdS, ZnS, $ZrO_2$, $TiO_2$, $SiO_2$, $Fe_2O_3$, Pt, Au, Cu etc., respectively.

***Biosynthesis of Nanoparticles***

Nature has devised various processes for the synthesis of nano and micro- length scaled inorganic materials which have contributed to the development of relatively new and largely unexplored area of research based on the biosynthesis of nanomaterials. Synthesis using bio-organisms is compatible with the green chemistry principles. "Green synthesis" of nanoparticles makes use of environmental friendly, non-toxic and safe reagents. Phytomining is the use of hyper accumulating plants to extract a metal from soil with recovery of the metal from the biomass to return an economic profit. Extracellular nano particle synthesis using plant leaf extracts rather than whole plants would be more economical owing to the easier downstream processing. Pioneering works on nano particles synthesis using plant extracts have been carried out by Sastry and others who reported that nano particles can be synthesized using plant extracts at rates comparable to those of chemical methods. The shape of nano particles plays a crucial role in the modulation of their optical properties.

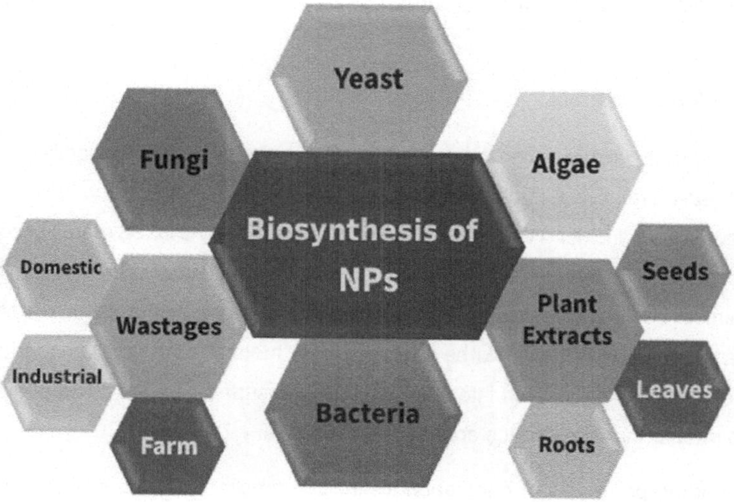

***Characterization techniques***

Characterization of nanoparticles is done using a variety of techniques, mainly drawn from materials science. The common techniques used to characterize the nanoparticles are given below:

| | |
|---|---|
| Scanning electron microscopy (SEM) | Morphology |
| Transmission electron microcopy (TEM) | Morphology and Size |
| Atomic force microscopy (AFM) | Surface property |
| Dynamic light scattering (DLS) | Optical property |
| X-ray photoelectron spectroscopy (XPS) | Elemental analysis |
| Powder X-ray diffraction (XRD) | Crystalline and Crystal structure |
| Ultraviolet-visible spectroscopy (UV-vis) | Optical properties |
| Photoluminescence (PL) spectroscopy | Optical properties |

***Properties of Nanomaterials***

Two principle factors cause the properties of nanomaterials to differ significantly from other materials: increased relative surface area and quantum effects. To understand the effect of particle size on surface area, consider a U.S. silver dollar. The silver contains 26.96 grams of coin silver has a diameter of about 40 mm and has a total surface area of approximately 27.70 square centimeters. If the same amount of coin silver divided into tiny particles - say one nanometer in diameter-the total surface area of those particles would be 11,400 square meters. When the amount of coin silver contained I silver dollar is rendered into 1nm particles, the surface area of those particles is 4.115 million times greater than the surface area of the silver dollar.

Some of the properties of nanomaterials include mechanical, thermal, electrical, melting, magnetic, catalytic, diffusive, and optical properties. Nanomaterials exhibit these unique properties as compared to their bulk counterpart. The reason behind nanomaterials exhibiting such specific properties is attributed to their size.

Some of the major properties of nanomaterials are:

***Electrical properties***

The electrical properties of nanomaterials vary between metallic to semiconducting materials. It depends on the diameter of nanomaterials. The very high electrical conductivity of nanomaterial is due to minimum defects in the structure. Nanomaterials have lower thermal and electrical conductivities than bulk materials. The classical free electron theory of metals states that the movement of electrons within a metallic solid lead to electrical conductivity. Nanomaterials have a high density of grain boundaries, which makes electric-phonon and phonon-phonon scattering effective and reduces conductivity.

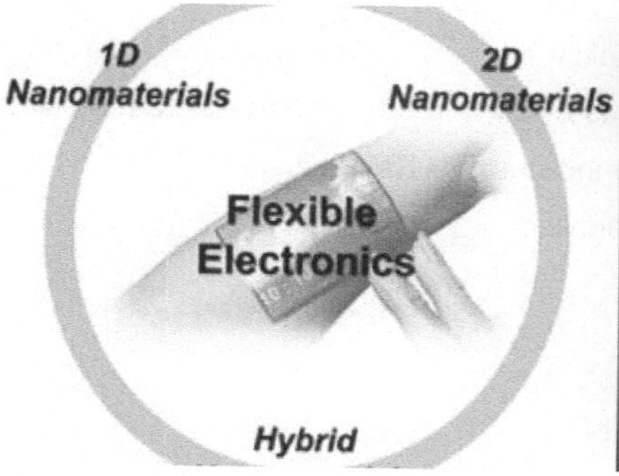

***Thermal conductivity***

The thermal conductivity of nanomaterials are very high, is due to the vibrational of covalent bonds. Its thermal conductivity is 10 times greater than the metal. The very high thermal conductivity of nanomaterials is also due to minimum defects in the structure. Due to the high density of defects compared to bulk materials, nanostructured materials have a higher thermal expansion coefficient, which measures how the size of the material changes as a function of temperature.

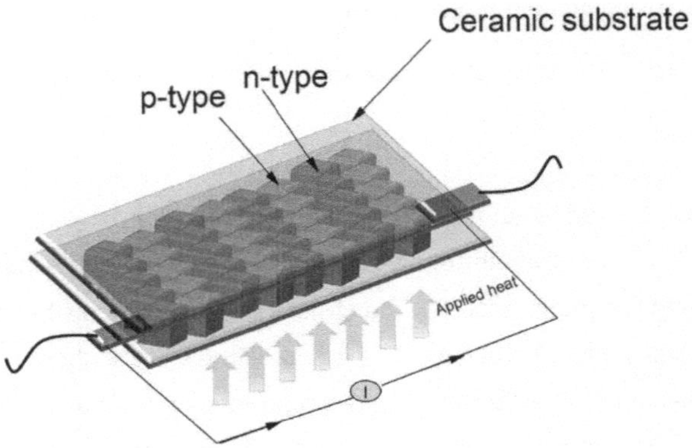


### ***Mechanical properties of nanomaterials***

Nanomaterials are very strong and withstand extreme strain. Most of the materials fracture on bending because of the presence of more defects, but nanomaterials possess only few defects in the structure. The unique mechanical properties of nanomaterials are due to the increased number of surface atoms and interfaces, which in turn leads to increased density of defects like grain boundaries, dislocations, triple junctions, etc. Nanomaterials exhibit the following mechanical properties as compared to bulk materials:

1. Increased strength
2. Increased toughness
3. Increased hardness
4. Increased ductility
5. Decreased elasticity

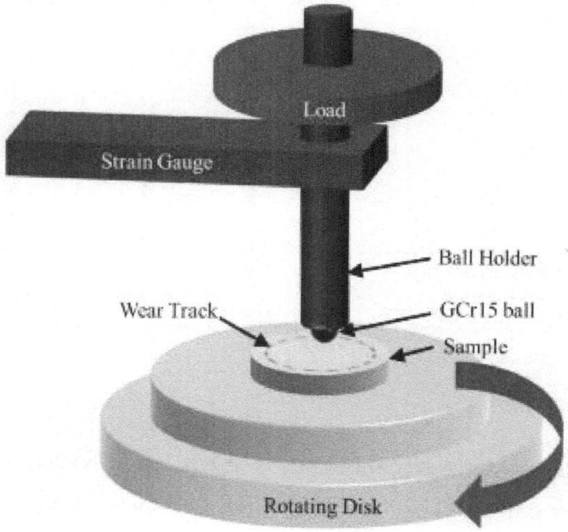


***Melting point of nanomaterials**:* Nanostructured materials have higher proportions of atoms on the surface and at grain boundaries than in the interior as compared to bulk materials, and the number of surface atoms rises with decreasing size. When an atom's vibrational amplitude exceeds its bond length, melting of the substance occurs.

When heat is applied, the atoms in the surface and grain boundaries vibrate more readily than the atoms in the interior, allowing melting to start on the surface and spread to the interior. This characteristic causes the melting point of a freely standing nanomaterial to be lower than that of bulk material. In the presence of nanomaterial, a matrix exerts pressure that limits the oscillation of surface atoms. Nanomaterial will have a greater melting point than bulk material under these circumstances.

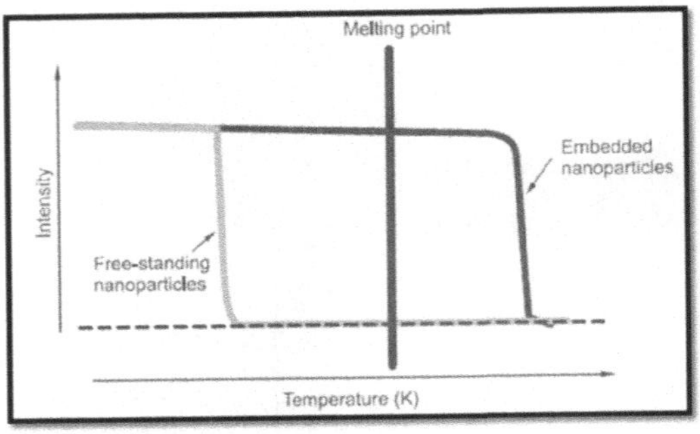


### *Catalytic properties*

Due to their larger surface nanoparticles made of transition element oxides exhibit interesting catalytic properties. In special cases, catalysis may be enhanced and more specific by decorating these particles with gold and platinum clusters. The surface area of a substance affects its catalytic activity. A study reveals that the percentage of surface atoms rises exponentially as size decreases. Greater surface area due to an increased fraction of surface atoms exerts stronger catalytic activity than bulk material.

### *Magnetic properties*

In magnetic nanoparticles, the energy of magnetic anisotropy may be that the small vector of magnetization fluctuates thermally: this is called superparamagnetism. Such a material is free of eminence and coercitivity. Touching superparamagnetic particles are losing this free special property by interaction, except the particles are kept at distance. Combining particles with high energy of anisotropy with superparamagnetic ones leads to a new class of permanent magnetic materials. Materials with nanostructures have higher saturation magnetization and magnetic coercivity values. If the external magnetic field is unable to further alter the magnetization of a material, it is said to be in a magnetically saturated state. The amount of magnetic field required to get a ferromagnetic material's saturation magnetization to zero is known as magnetic coercivity. Coercivity and saturation magnetization are both used to measure a magnet's strength. Due to the lowered size effect, the value of both of these attributes has increased. Small particles have a single magnetic domain behavior that is easily aligned by an external magnet, giving rise to improved magnetic properties.

***Optical properties***

In small nano clusters the effect of reduced dimensionality on electronic structure has the most profound effect on the energies of highest occupied molecular orbital (HOMO) which is valence band and the lowest unoccupied molecular orbital (LUMO), essentially the conduction band.

When compared to bulk materials, nanomaterials exhibit distinctive optical characteristics such as greater scattering, absorption, and luminescence. The shape and size of nanoparticles can be altered to change their optical properties. Such unique optical properties can be explained by considering Quantum confinement and surface plasmon effects:

***Quantum Confinement:*** Quantum confinement is a prominent effect in semiconducting materials having one dimension in the range of 1-10nm. In bulk materials, the exciton-Bohr radius (exciton is the electron-hole pairs present in a material and the distance of separation between them is the exciton-Bohr radius) is much smaller than the size of bulk material, while in the case of semiconducting material, the exciton-Bohr radius is smaller or comparable to the size of bulk material. Thus, it is confined since exciton cannot extend to its natural limit. This phenomenon is called quantum confinement. Due to this effect, the energy level of both the valence band and conduction band becomes discrete, and the band gap energy changes significantly in comparison to the bulk material. The larger the size of nanomaterial, the smaller will be the band gap energy and vice-versa. This results in a blue shift in optical property.

***Surface plasmon effect:*** Similar to how photons are created by quantizing light and sound waves, plasmons are quasiparticles created by quantizing plasma oscillations. Another quasiparticle known as a plasma polariton can be produced when plasmons combine with a photon. Surface plasmons (SP) are types of plasmons that are restricted to surfaces and interact with light intensely to produce polariton. SPs are responsible for the nanomaterial's color. When the size of the metallic particle becomes smaller than the wavelength of light and the natural oscillation frequency of the plasmon becomes equal to the frequency of light used, then the surface plasmon is excited or resonance is achieved called the surface plasmon effect. For example, the frequency for spherical gold particles is roughly 0.58 times that of bulk plasma. Consequently, the SP frequency is in the visible range even though the bulk plasma frequency is in the UV region (wavelength close to 520nm). If a wave of light is applied to a suspension of nanoparticles in a host, the local electric field may be greatly amplified close to an SP resonance.

**Diffusivity**: Nanostructured materials have more interfaces than bulk materials since they are smaller. The interface offers simple diffusion pathways. Therefore, self-diffusion along the defect side is more effective in nanostructured materials than in their bulk analog.

## Applications of Nanotechnology

Below we list some key applications of nanomaterials. Most current applications represent evolutionary developments of existing technologies: for example, the reduction in size of electronics devices.

### *Sunscreens and Cosmetics*

The traditional chemical UV protection approach suffers from its poor long-term stability. A sunscreen based on mineral nanoparticles such as titanium dioxide offer several advantages. Titanium oxide nanoparticles have a comparable UV protection property. Nano-sized titanium dioxide and zinc oxide are currently used in some sunscreens, as they absorb and reflect ultraviolet (UV) rays, yet are transparent to visible light, and so are more appealing to the consumer. Nano-sized iron oxide is present in some lipsticks as a pigment. The use of nanoparticles in cosmetics has raised a number of concerns about consumer safety.

### *Paints*

Incorporating nanoparticles in paints could improve their performance, for example by making them lighter and giving them different properties. Thinner paint coatings ('light weighting'), used for example on aircraft, would reduce their weight, which could be beneficial to the environment.

***Displays***

The huge market for large area, high brightness, flat-panel displays as used in television screens and computer monitors is driving the development of some nanomaterials. Nanocrystalline zinc selenide, zinc sulphide, cadmium sulphide and lead telluride synthesized by sol gel techniques are candidates for the next generation of light-emitting phosphors.

***Batteries and capacitors***

With the growth in portable electronic equipment (mobile phones, laptop computers, remote sensors), there is great demand for lightweight, high-energy density batteries. Nanocrystalline materials synthesized by sol–gel techniques are candidates for separator plates in batteries because of their foam-like (aerogel) structure, which can hold considerably more energy than conventional ones. Nickel–metal hydride batteries made of nanocrystalline nickel and metal hydrides are envisioned to require less frequent recharging and to last longer because of their large surface area.

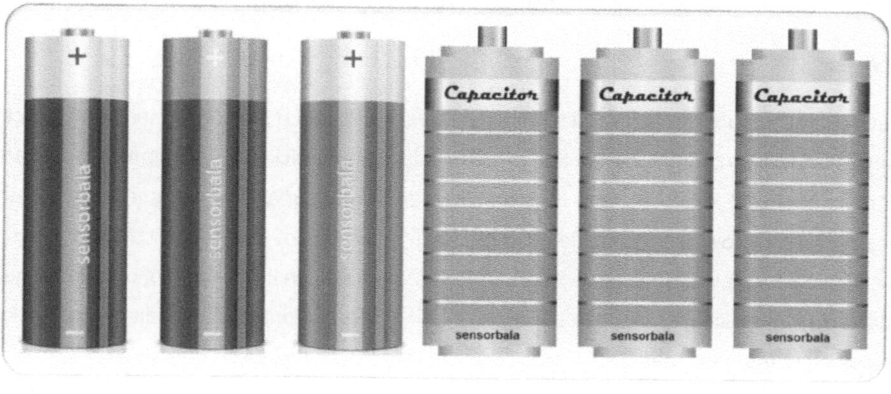

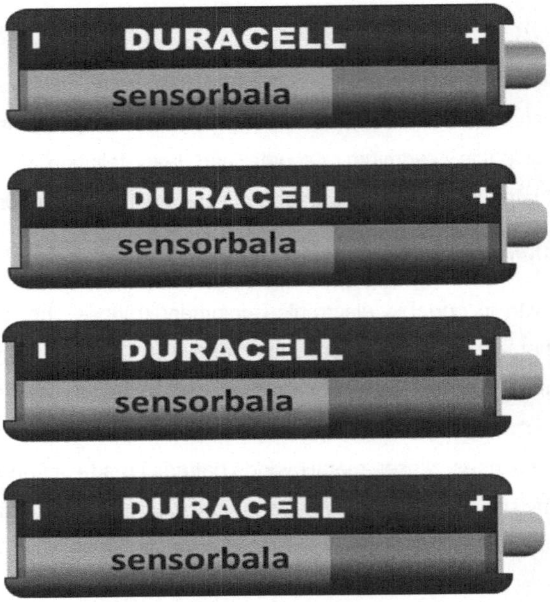


***Catalysis***

In general, nanoparticles have a high surface area, and hence provide higher catalytic activity. Catalysis is important for the production of chemicals. Nanoparticles serve as an efficient catalyst for some chemical reaction, due to the extremely large surface to volume ratio. Platinum nanoparticles are now being considered in the next generation of automotive catalytic converters because the very high surface area of nanoparticles could reduce the amount of platinum required. Some chemical reactions are also carried out using nanomaterials. For example, reduction of nickel oxide to the base metal Ni.

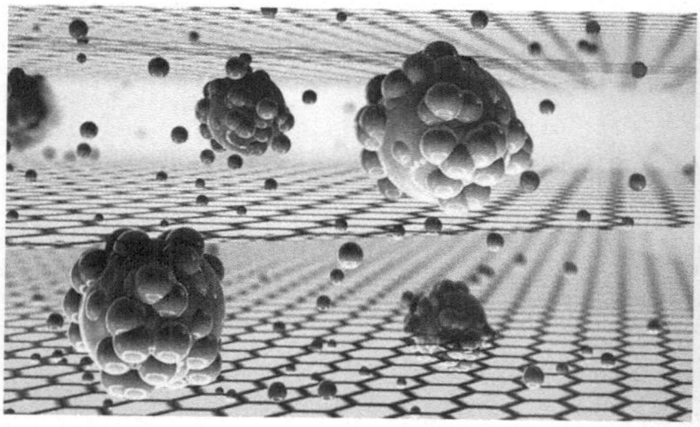

***Medicine***

Nanotechnology has been a boon in medical field by delivering drugs to specific cells using nanoparticles. The overall drug consumption and side effects can be lowered significantly by depositing the active agent in the morbid region only and in no higher dose than needed. This highly selective approach reduces costs and human suffering. Nanotechnology can also help to reproduce or to repair damaged tissue. “Tissue engineering” might replace today's conventional treatments like organ transplants or artificial implants. For example, bones can be regrown on carbon nanotube scaffolds.

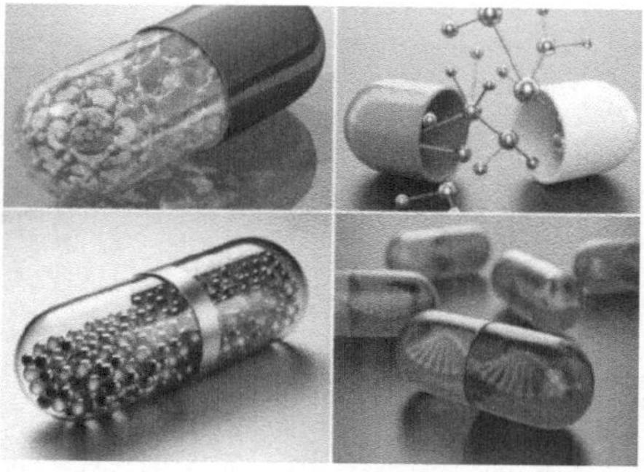

***Gas Sensors and detectors***

The gases like $NO_2$ and $NH_3$ can be detected based on increase in electrical conductivity of nanomaterials. This is attributed to increase in hole concentration in nanomaterials due to charge transfer from nanomaterials to $NO_2$ as the gas molecules bind the nanomaterials.

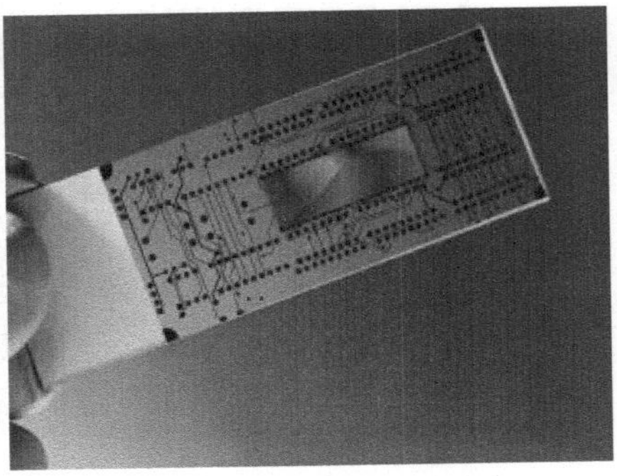

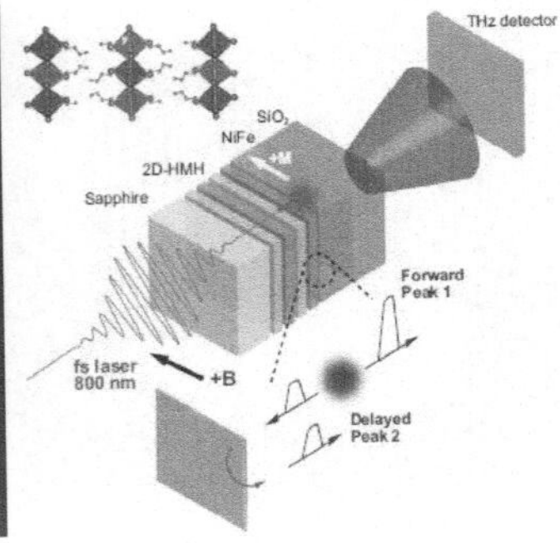


***Food***

Nanotechnology can be applied in the production, processing, safety and packaging of food. A nanocomposite coating process could improve food packaging by placing anti-microbial agents directly on the surface of the coated film. New foods are among the nanotechnology created consumer products coming onto the market at the rate of 3 to 4 per week. According to company information posted on PEN's Web site, the canola oil, by Shemen Industries of Israel, contains an additive called "nano-drops" designed to carry vitamins, minerals and phytochemicals through the digestive system and urea.

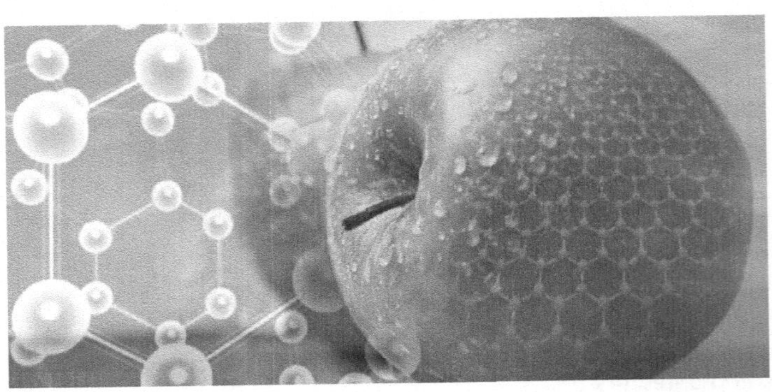

***Construction***

Nanotechnology has the potential to make construction faster, cheaper and safer. Automation of nanotechnology construction can allow for the creation of structures from advanced homes to massive skyscrapers much more quickly and at much lower cost. The Silica ($SiO_2$) is present in conventional concrete as part of the normal mix. When nano silica is added to concrete the particle packing can be improved mechanical properties. The addition of nano silica to cement based materials can also control the degradation of the fundamental C-S-H (calcium silicate hydrate) reaction of concrete caused by calcium leaching in water as well as block water penetration and therefore lead to improvements in durability. The strength of concrete can also be increase by adding haematite ($Fe_2O_3$) nanoparticles.

Steel has been widely available material and has a major role in the construction industry. The use of nanotechnology in steel helps to improve the properties of steel. The nano size steel produce stronger steel cables, which can be used in bridge construction.

The glass is also an important material in construction. There is a lot of research being carried out on the application of nanotechnology to glass. Titanium dioxide ($TiO_2$) nanoparticles are used to coat glazing since it has sterilizing and anti-fouling properties. The particles catalyze powerful reactions which breakdown organic pollutants, volatile organic compounds and bacterial membranes. Most of glass in construction is on the exterior surface of buildings. Therefore, the light and heat entering the building through glass has to be prevented. The nanotechnology can provide a better solution to block light and heat coming through windows.

Coatings is an important area in construction. Coatings are extensively use to paint the walls, doors and windows. Coatings should provides a protective layer which is bound to the base material to produce a surface of the desired protective or functional properties. Nanotechnology is being applied to paints to obtained the coatings having self healing capabilities and corrosion protection under insulation. Since these coatings are hydrophobic and repels water from the metal pipe and can also protect metal from salt water attack.

### *Agriculture*

Applications of nanotechnology have the potential to change the entire agriculture sector and food industry from production to conservation, processing, packaging, nanofertilizers, transportation and even waste treatment.

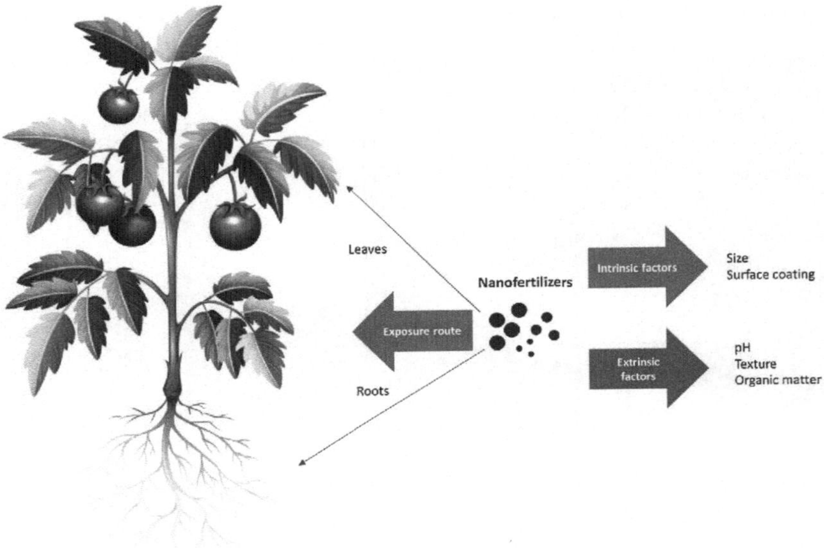


### *Energy*

The most advanced nanotechnology projects related to energy are; storage, conversion, manufacturing improvements by reducing materials and process rates, energy saving and enhanced renewable energy sources. Today's best solar cells have layers of several different semiconductors stacked together to absorb light at different energies but they still only manage to use 40 percent of the Sun's energy. Commercially available solar cells have much lower efficiencies (15-20%). Nanotechnology could help increase the efficiency of light conversion by using nanostructures.

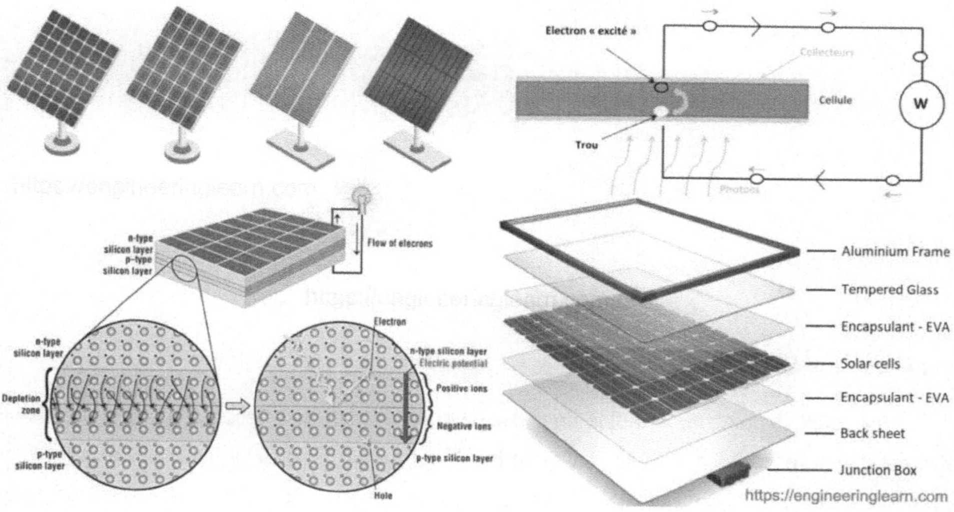


### *Other Applications*

Some commercial products on the market today utilizing nanomaterials include stain resistant textiles and reinforced tennis rackets. Companies like Kraft foods are heavily funding nanomaterials based plastic packaging. Food will stay fresh longer if the packaging is less permeable to atmosphere. Coors Brewing company has developed new plastic beer bottles that stay cold for longer periods.

### *Silver Phosphate ($Ag_3PO_4$)*

Metal nanoparticles have found, due to their antibacterial properties, application in medicine where bacterial sterility is required. Especially, during transplantations, implants represent a high risk of bacterial infection. To minimize this threat, the utilization of nanoparticles in combination with certain polymeric substances was found very effective. Complexes of polymer materials with silver nanoparticles are widely used as growth inhibitors G+ and G- bacteria, and as substances utilized for posttraumatic or postoperative tissue regeneration applications.

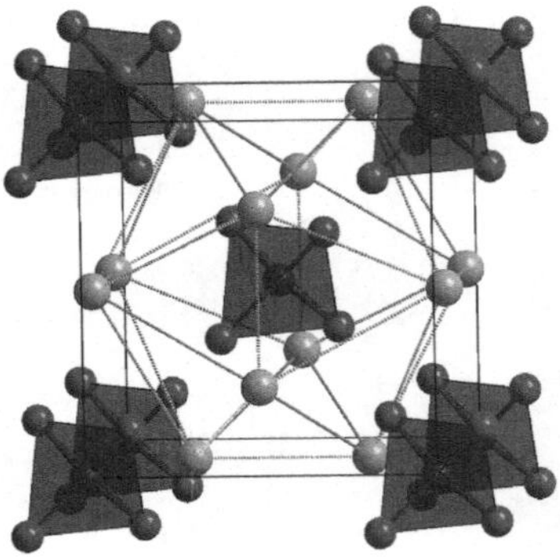

Crystalline structure of silver phosphate

***Application of Silver Phosphate***

As well as being important in analytical chemistry, the precipitation of silver phosphate is also used in silver staining of biological materials (after reduction to silver metal)-as a magnifying agent for phosphate. Silver phosphate also found use in early photography as a light sensitive agent.

In 2010, silver phosphate was reported as having a high (90%) quantum yield as a photocatalyst for the visible light photochemical splitting of water, and for production of activated oxygen by the same method. Silver phosphate is also a potential material for incorporating silver ion antibacterial properties into materials.

Silver phosphate is a semiconductor studied in environmental chemistry due to its photocatalytic abilities. When excited by radiation in the UV-Vis range (< 530nm), electrons from the valence band of oxygen atoms are displaced, creating positively-charged holes (*i.e.*, sites from a full valence band with one electron absent) where organic contaminants can be degraded. As a secondary effect, the silver cations scavenge the excited electrons and are reduced to metallic silver. Dental composites polymerized by visible light typically employ camphor Quinone as photo initiator, which has a maximum absorption peak of 470nm wavelength. Therefore, it can be hypothesized that radiation emitted by dental light curing units could effectively promote the formation of metallic silver nanoparticles *in situ*, by the reduction of $Ag^+$ from $Ag_3PO_4$.

Silver phosphate ($Ag_3PO_4$), also known as silver orthophosphate, is a water-insoluble yellow chemical compound produced from the interaction of soluble silver salt with orthophosphate. Silver phosphate precipitation is similarly utilized in silver staining of biological materials as a phosphate-enlarging agent and as a light-sensitive agent in early photography, besides its antibacterial effects. $Ag_3PO_4$ is a photocatalyst driven by visible light. It displays a band gap energy equal to 2.43eV. Pristine $Ag_3PO_4$ photocatalyst may absorb solar light energy with wavelengths less than 530 nm and has a VB close to +2.9V compared to a standard hydrogen electrode (SHE, pH=0), indicating an exceptional oxidizing capability. Furthermore, silver phosphate has an extraordinary quantum yield (90%) for photo-chemically splitting water under visible light and generating activated oxygen by the same technique.

***Copper Oxide***

Copper (II)-oxide nanoparticles (CuO-NPs) belongs to monoclinic structure system. It has wide different applications according to the physical and chemical properties, such as superconductivity, photovoltaic properties, relatively stable, low cost and the antimicrobial activity.

Copper oxide (CuO) is one of potential p-type semiconductors and gains considerable attentions due to its excellent optical, electrical, physical, and magnetic properties. CuO with narrow band gap of 1.2eV is extensively used in various applications such as catalysis, solar energy conversion, gas sensor and field emission. However, these novel properties can be improved by synthesis in CuO nanostructures that shown excellent performance comparing to bulk counterpart. Different nanostructures of CuO are synthesized in form of nanowire, nano-rod, nano-needle, nano-flower and nanoparticle. In the past decades, various methods have been proposed to produce CuO nanoparticles with different sizes and shapes such as thermal oxidation, sonochemical, combustion and quick-precipitation.

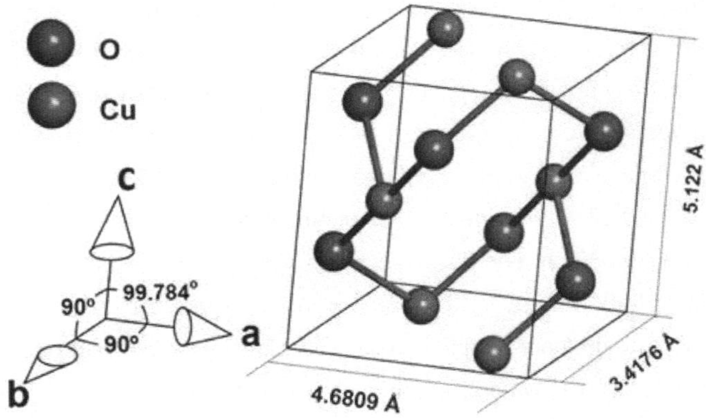


Crystalline Structure of Copper Oxide

**Applications of Copper Oxides**

Applications of CuO-NPs nowadays are very important for antioxidant, antibacterial, thermal conductivity, catalytic, battery and solar cells applications.

***Environmental pollution***

Environmental nanotechnology is considered to play a key role in the shaping of current environmental engineering and science. Looking at the nanoscale has stimulated the development and use of novel and cost-effective technologies for remediation, pollution detection, catalysis and others. However, there is also a wide debate about the safety of nanoparticles and their potential impact on environment and biota, not only among scientists but also the public. Especially the new field of nano-toxicology has received a lot of attention in recent years. Maintaining and re-improving the quality of water, air and soil, so that the Earth will be able to support human and other life sustainably, are one of the great challenges of our time. The scarcity of water, in terms of both quantity and quality, poses a significant threat to the well-being of people, especially in developing countries.

### *Nanotechnology and pollution control*

Pollution results from resource production and consumption, which in their current state are very wasteful. Nanofabrication holds much potential for effective pollution control, but it currently faces many problems that prevent it from mass commercialization particularly its high cost. Nanotechnology plays a vital role in air and water pollution control.

### *Air Pollution*

Air pollution can be remediated using nanotechnology in several ways. One is through the use of nano-catalysts with increased surface area for gaseous reactions. Catalysts work by speeding up chemical reactions that transform harmful vapors from cars and industrial plants into harmless gases. Catalysts currently in use include a nanofiber catalyst made of manganese oxide that removes volatile organic compounds from industrial smokestacks.

### *Water Pollution*

As with air pollution, harmful pollutants in water can be converted into harmless chemicals through chemical reactions. Trichloroethene, a dangerous pollutant commonly found in industrial wastewater, can be catalyzed and treated by nanoparticles. Studies have shown that these materials should be highly suitable as hydro dehalogenation and reduction catalysts for the remediation of various organic and inorganic groundwater contaminants.

***Dyes***

Dyes are colored organic compounds that are used to impart color to various substrates, including paper, leather, fur, hair, drugs, cosmetics, waxes, greases, plastics and textile materials. The two major types of colorants produced today are dyes and pigments. Pigments both inorganic and organic types (Figure) are almost applied in an aggregated or crystalline in soluble form that requires a binder to form a coating on the surface of a substrate. The color intensity of the dye molecule depends on how strongly it absorbs radiation in the visible region, which extends from 400 to 700nm.

Organic Dyes

***Physio-Chemical Water Treatment***

Physicochemical wastewater treatment techniques are applied for the removal of heavy metals, oils and greases, suspended matter and emulgating organic substances, organic and an organic component, difficult to decompose, non-polar organic substances, toxic pollutants or high salt concentrations, phosphorus. The physicochemical wastewater treatment techniques are used as pretreatment, final treatment as well as specific treatment for wastewater reuse as process water.

**Used Techniques**

- flocculation
- coagulation

- flotation
- neutralization
- electro flotation
- membrane technology-membrane filtration
- $NH_3$ stripper-absorbers
- sludge treatment

### *Advanced Oxidation Processes*

Advanced oxidation processes (abbreviation: AOPs), in a broad sense, refers to a set of chemical treatment procedures designed to remove organic (and sometimes inorganic) materials in water and waste water by oxidation through reactions with hydroxyl radicals ($\cdot OH$). In real-world applications of wastewater treatment, however, this term usually refers more specifically to a subset of such chemical processes that employ ozone ($O_3$), hydrogen peroxide ($H_2O_2$) and/or UV light. The AOP is usually used for removing contaminants from wastewater coming out of several types of heavy industries like:

- Petrochemical & Plastic Industry
- Chemical Industry.
- Food Processing Industry.
- Pharmaceutical Industry.
- Metal and Metal Plating Industry.
- Textile and Dying Industry

# Chapter-2

## Facile Synthesis and Characterization of Nanowire-like Copper Oxide Electrodes for Sensitive Electrochemical Sensing of Paracetamol

***Summary***

Development of nanomaterials for efficiently detecting pharmaceutical drugs such as paracetamol (PRT) is important for industrial applications. In this study, we synthesized copper oxide nanowire (CuO NW) via simple chemical co-precipitation technique. The prepared CuO NW electrodes were coated on a glassy carbon electrode (GCE) for conducting sensitive and selective electrochemical detection of PRT. The CuO NW electrodes were systematically characterized using various spectroscopic techniques including X-ray diffraction, Fourier transform infrared spectroscopy, energy dispersive X-ray analysis, and field emission scanning electron microscopy. The electrochemical properties of CuO NW electrodes were verified using electrochemical impedance spectroscopy and voltammetry techniques. As an electrochemical sensor, the proposed nanowire-like copper oxide–glassy carbon electrode (CuO NW/GCE) demonstrated an excellent sensitivity with a limit of detection was 10nM. Furthermore, the CuO NW/GCE displays a wider linear response range (0.1–275μM). The electrode also has high selectivity. The selectivity was tested in the presence of three different substances. Finally, the CuO NW/GCE exhibits consistent durability, reproducibility, and repeatability, which are important parameters for future development as a point-of-care device. Transition metal oxides are crucial materials for magnetic storage media, solar energy transformation, electronics, and catalysis. Some transition metal oxides, such as zinc oxide, titanium dioxide, and iron oxide, have been proven to be potential candidates for many applications. Among all transition metal oxides, copper oxide (CuO) is categorized as a highly attractive metal oxide semiconductor material because of its superior performance in electronic and optoelectronic industrial applications such as gas sensing device fabrication, semiconductors, and thin films for photovoltaic cells. CuO is an abundantly available material and is nonhazardous. The narrow band gap energy of CuO is 2.0 eV. Furthermore, the fabrication and processing of CuO entails low cost. Several synthetic approaches have been recently reported for the preparation of CuO nanostructures such as thermal oxidation of copper foil, hydrothermal synthesis, vapor-phase solid preparation, ultrasonic irradiation method, thermal decomposition of precursors, and electron beam lithography. However, it is still a challenge to develop a simple, rapid, easy to control, and energy-efficient method for manufacturing CuO nanostructures with a designable morphology on a large scale. To date, various morphological CuO nanostructures have been synthesized through facile solution methods such as ribbon-like films, nanowires, nanorods, plate-like powder, hollow microspheres, and nanorods bundles.

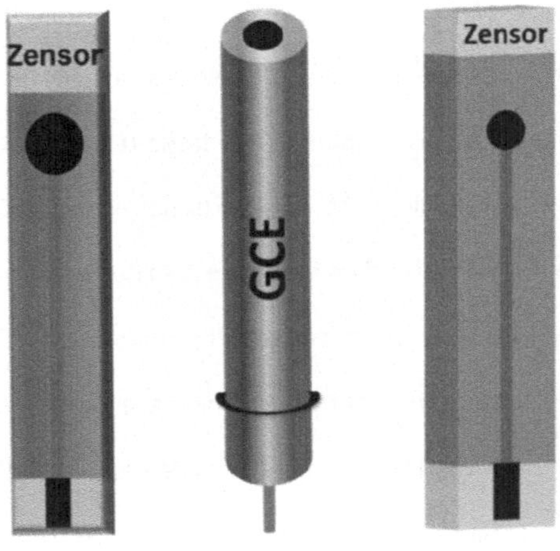

Acetaminophen or paracetamol (PRT, N-acetyl-p-aminophenol) is widely used as an analgesic and antipyretic agent. PRT is utilized extensively for relieving moderate fever associated with a headache, backache, arthritis, and postoperative pain. In general, PRT seems to be dangerous even when consumed in normal therapeutic doses and may create serious side effects such as hepatotoxicity and nephrotoxicity, which are related to liver and kidney damage. Therefore, the development of a simple, a fast, a sensitive, and an accurate method for the determination of PRT is crucial for quality control in pharmaceutical and overdose diagnosis.

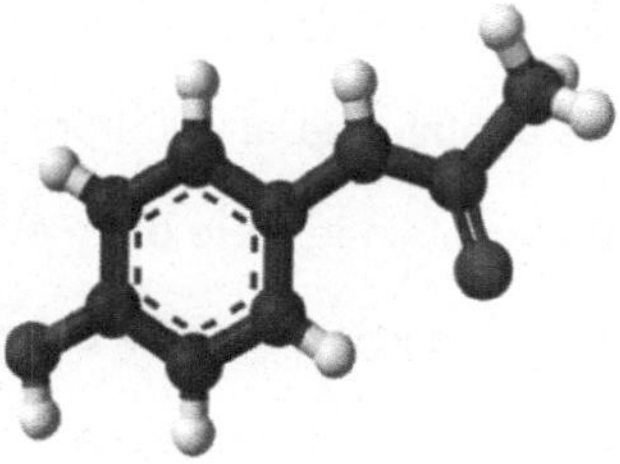

Numerous techniques have been utilized for detecting PRT in biological fluids and pharmaceutical formulations such as chromatography, chemiluminescence, capillary electrophoresis, spectrophotometry, titrimetry, flow injection methods, and electrochemistry. The electrochemical technique is more efficient than all aforementioned methods and is the most widely applied because it has the following characteristics: higher sensitivity, higher selectivity, faster response, easier to operate, and inexpensive. In the present work, I report a facile chemical precipitation method for large-scale production of CuO NW electrodes. The formation mechanism of CuO NW electrodes was confirmed. The paracetamol electrochemical sensing properties of CuO NW electrodes were systematically studied.

### *Synthesis of CuO nanowires*

CuO NW electrodes were synthesized through a chemical precipitation method. First, 0.6M (4.788g) $CuSO_4$ was dissolved in 50mL purified water. Moreover, 0.6 M (1.1999g) sodium hydroxide (NaOH) was dissolved in 50mL purified water. Then, both the solutions were mixed in a round-bottomed flask by conducting magnetic stirring at 400 rpm for 4 h. Subsequently, NaOH was added in a dropwise manner with continuous stirring. The resulting as-prepared solution was performed to sedimentation for 24 hrs, and the obtained precipitate was washed thoroughly several times with purified water. Then, ethanol was added to the purified precipitate, and the mixture was centrifuged at 4000rpm for 30min. Subsequently, the resultant brown precipitates that were obtained were dried at 60°C in a hot air oven for consecutive 6 h. Then, the precipitate was calcined at 400°C for 2hrs and finely ground using a mortar and a pestle. Finally, experiments and electrochemical studies were conducted at room temperature on the prepared sample. The explored the preparation of CuO nanowires and its electrochemical sensor application.

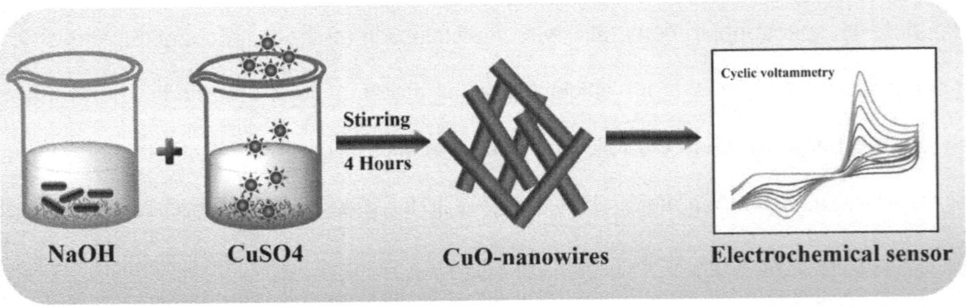


Synthesis of CuO-nanowire via chemical precipitation method.

### *Preparation of nanowire-like copper oxide-glassy carbon electrode (CuO-NW/GCE)*

To fabricate a PRT sensor, a glassy carbon electrode (GCE) was polished using 0.05 μM alumina slurry and then ultrasonicated for approximately 5min in ethanol and purified water successively to remove the alumina slurry adsorbed on the surface of the GCE. Moreover, 3mg of as-synthesized CuO NW electrodes was dispersed in 1mL purified water, and the mixture was sonicated for 30min. Then, 8μL of the dispersed solution was drop coated on the surface of the cleaned GCE. Subsequently, the GCE was dried in an oven at 55°C for 30min. The following figure Depicts the fabrication of the CuO NWs modified GC electrodes.

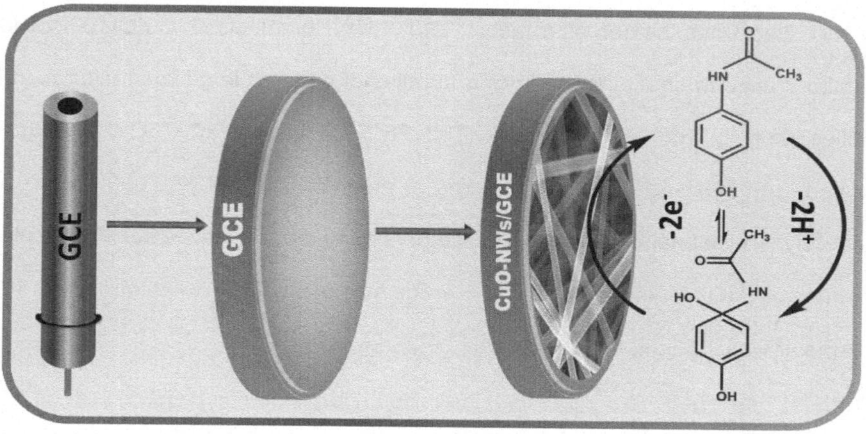


Fabrication and electrochemical oxidation of PRT at CuO-NWs modified electrode

### *Measurement of PRT*

The electrocatalytic performance of different films toward the oxidation of PRT was investigated by conducting CV tests on a 0.1M phosphate buffer (pH 7) at a scan rate of 0.05 $V \cdot s^{-1}$ at room temperature. Different concentrations of PRT ranging from 25 to 150μM were detected using the proposed CuO NW/GCE, and the linear plot was used to determine the peak current (μA) versus the PRT concentration (μM). To sustain the reproducibility of the electrode, it is kept in a refrigerator at 4ºC and immersed in a 0.1M phosphate buffer solution (pH 7) every time it is removed from the refrigerator.

## Data collection and Interpretation

### *Morphological and composition analysis of CuO NW electrodes*

The surface morphology of CuO NW electrodes was confirmed using field emission scanning electron microscopy (FE-SEM) images recorded at different magnifications Figure (A) and (B) display the FE-SEM image at a low-magnification (X15,000 and X35,000) of CuO NW electrodes before calcination. The newly synthesized $Cu(OH)_2$ individually presented a uniform structure comprising bundles of crushed leaf-like structures in huge quantities ranging from 0.6 to 1.0μm. The FE-SEM images of CuO NW electrodes presented in Fig(C) and (D) were captured at magnifications of X50,000 and X65,000, respectively. These images display a bundle of huge number of nanowires and display the active sites of CuO NW electrodes. The average size of a CuO NW electrode was 100nm, the diameter was 1.32nm, and length was 56.23nm.

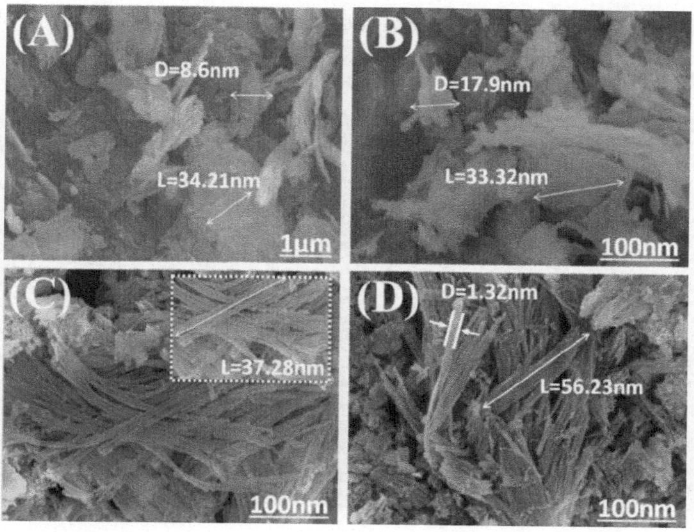


SEM images of CuO NWs

Simultaneously, energy dispersive X-ray (EDX) analysis for CuO NW electrodes was conducted at 10 keV. The analysis results clearly presented the presence of copper (Cu) and oxygen (O) elements in the CuO NW electrode. These data indicated that the nanoparticles are merely stoichiometric. The weight percentages of copper and oxygen calculated using the EDX analysis were 30.09% oxygen and 69.91% copper before calcination and 22.67% oxygen and 77.33% copper after calcination. The EDX analysis revealed the presence of copper and oxygen at an atomic ratio from 1% to 1.71% before the calcination of CuO NW electrodes and from 1% to 1.15% after the calcination of CuO NW electrodes. The results have a strong confirmation of CuO NW electrodes. A previous study confirmed the formation of the as-prepared CuO, actively $Cu(OH)_2$ before calcination and CuO NW electrodes after.

To determine the location of Cu and O, elemental mapping of the CuO NW electrode was conducted. The results obtained by analyzing, suggested that Cu and O colocalized with the CuO NW electrodes before calcination (Figure (A)-(C)) and after calcination (Figure (D)-(F)).

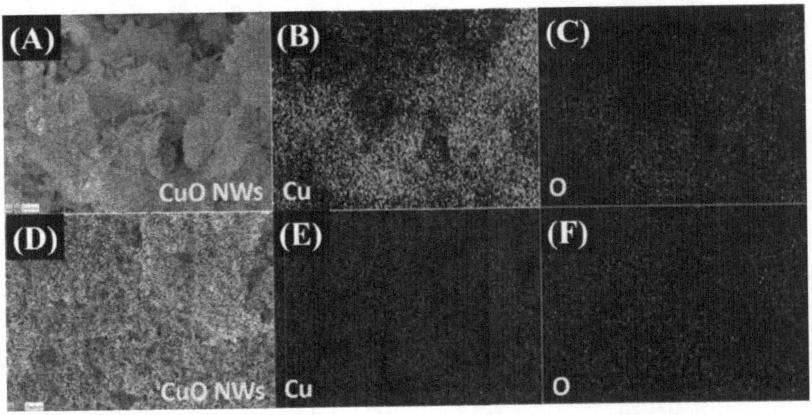


Elemental mapping of as-synthesized CuO NWs, the compositions of Cu and O distribution before (A-C) and after calcination (D-F)

***Crystalline structure analysis of CuO NW electrodes***

The crystalline structure and phase purity of CuO NW electrodes were characterized using X-ray diffraction (XRD). Figure (A) presents the XRD patterns of the $Cu(OH)_2$ complex obtained after drying the precipitate at 50°C. The diffraction peaks at 32.46°, 35.51°, 38.71°, 44.75°, 48.79°, 53.44°, and 58.29° correspond to the $(\bar{1}10)$,$(\bar{1}11)$,(022),(111), (150),(020), and $(\bar{1}13)$ planes of orthorhombic $Cu(OH)_2$, respectively, (JCPDS 80-0656). The XRD patterns of CuO NW electrodes were obtained by annealing the electrodes to a temperature of 400°C. The peaks in the XRD patterns of CuO NW electrodes were compared with the peaks in the standard data. Figure(B) shows the major peaks at 2θ values of 32.75°, 35.55°, 38.85°, 48.75°, 53.85°, 58.35°, 61.55°, 66.45°, 68.15°, 72.45°, and 74.85° that corresponded to the (110),$(\bar{1}11)$,(200),$(\bar{2}02)$,(020),(202),$(\bar{1}13)$,(220),(311), and (004) planes, respectively. These XRD patterns can be attributed to the monoclinic CuO NW electrode crystal, which is in agreement with the standard JCPDS data (ref no.5-0661). No other characteristic peaks of impurities such as $Cu(OH)_2$, $Cu_2O$, or precursors were observed, thus indicating the formation of a pure phase CuO NW electrodes. The average crystal size of the CuO NW electrodes was examined using the full-width half-maximum (FWHM) value of a prominent diffraction peak of the XRD pattern through Scherer's equation as follows:

$$X_s = k\lambda | \beta \cos\theta \quad \rightarrow \qquad (1)$$

Where, Xs is the size of the crystal, λ is X-ray wavelength, ß is the FWHM of the diffraction peak, θ is the diffraction angle, and k is Scherer's constant. The crystal size was calculated for the diffraction plane (111), and the average size was found to be 20.1nm. The experimental results were similar to the diffraction pattern results of CuO NW electrodes reported in a previous study.

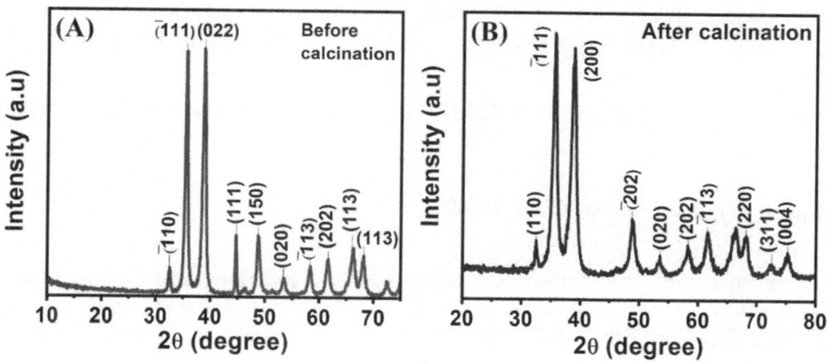


XRD patterns of as-synthesized CuO NWs (A) before calcination (B) after calcination

To determine the chemical and structural nature of the synthesized $Cu(OH)_2$ and CuO NW electrodes, the effect of the chemicals used in the Fourier transform infrared spectroscopy (FTIR) analysis was analyzed. Figure (A) and (b) represent the FTIR spectrum recorded for the $Cu(OH)_2$ and CuO NW electrodes, respectively, in the range of 400-4,000cm$^{-1}$ before and after calcination. In the as-synthesized $Cu(OH)_2$, the presence of peak at 3400.11cm$^{-1}$ indicates the stretching mode of the hydroxyl groups in $Cu(OH)_2$. The peak at 1707.71cm$^{-1}$ indicates the bending mode of the absorbed water in the as-synthesized $Cu(OH)_2$. In the FTIR spectrum, the

CuO NW electrode peaks at 837.36 and 1187.56cm$^{-1}$ correspond to strong Cu-O stretching vibrations. The peak at 1495.57cm$^{-1}$ corresponds to C=O stretching acidic groups. Bands at 3448.35cm$^{-1}$ may be attributed to the Cu-OH groups displayed in Figure (B).

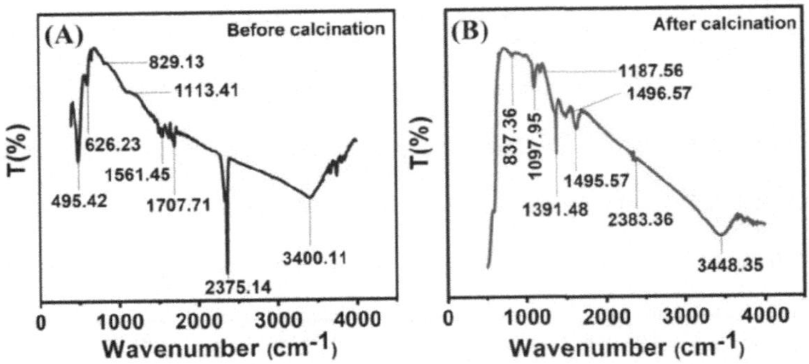


FTIR spectrum of as-synthesized CuO NWs (A) before calcination (B) after calcination at 400°C

***Electrochemical properties of CuO NW/GCE***

The electrochemical impedance spectroscopy (EIS) results of the unmodified GCE and CuO NW/GCE in 0.1M KCl containing 5mM $Fe(CN)_6^{3-/4-}$ were investigated. The applied frequency range was fixed at 100 MHz to 100 kHz. Figure displays the rate of the charge transfer reaction on the surface of the unmodified GCE and the CuO NW/GCE. The smaller semicircle curve of the CuO NW electrode indicates lower impedance, which supports easier electron transfer. The inset in Figure displays Randles equivalent circuit model. This model uses electrolyte resistance ($R_s$), charge transfer resistance ($R_{ct}$), double layer capacitance ($C_{dl}$), and Warburg impedance ($Z_w$) to fit the Nyquist plot. The semicircle of the EIS plot obtained for the CuO NW/GCE was 2.4 times higher than that of the plot obtained for the unmodified GCE. The corresponding $R_{ct}$ values were 98.31 for the unmodified GCE (Figure (a)) and 52.03 for the CuO NWs/GCE (Figure (b)). These results from the impedance analysis suggested that CuO NW electrodes are good conductive materials for constructing an electrochemical sensor.

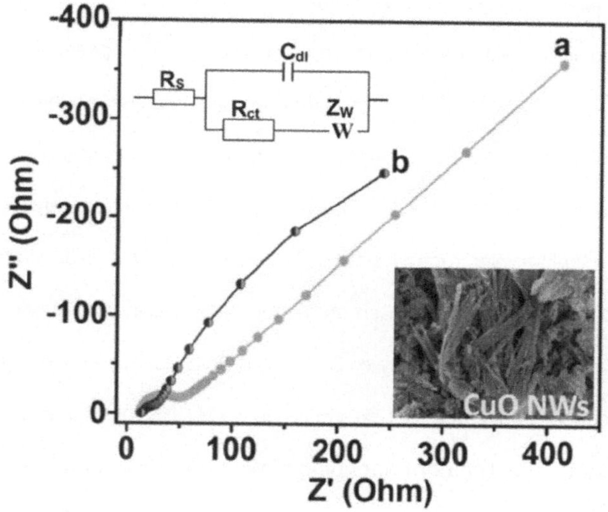


Typical Nyquist semicircle plots of EIS spectra. Electrode fabrication step measured in a mixture of 5mM of $[Fe(CN)_6]^{3-/4-}$ and 0.1M of KCl solutions at an applied amplitude of ± 5 mV within a frequency range of 0.01Hz-100MHz. (a) Bare GCE (b) CuO NWs modified GCE. Randles equivalent circuit model is shown in inset with the corresponding FESEM image of CuO NWs

***Detection of PRT using a CuO NWs/GCE***

The electrochemical oxidation properties of PRT (50 µM) obtained using the unmodified GCE and the CuO NW/GCE were studied using 0.1MPBS (pH 7) at a scan rate of 0.05 $Vs^{-1}$ by conducting CV tests. The unmodified GCE does not present any obvious redox behavior in the presence of 50µM PRT (Figure (a)), which indicates that the unmodified GCE is electrochemically inactive and it is not suitable for the detection of PRT in the selected potential range. Conversely, when the unmodified GCE was modified with CuO NW electrodes (50μM PRT), a quasi-reversible redox behavior with oxidation and reduction peak potentials of 0.49 V ($E_{pa}$) and 0.06 V ($E_{pc}$), respectively, was obtained (Figure (b)). The redox peak current of PRT obtained using the CuO NWs/GCE was due to the oxidation and reduction reactions that occurred due to two electrons and one proton transfer. The possible electrochemical redox mechanism of the CuO NWs/GCE is presented in Scheme. Moreover, the redox peak current obtained using CuO NWs/GCE is 6.5-fold higher than that obtained using unmodified GCE. This result suggests that the CuO NW/GCE had excellent electrocatalytic activity toward PRT detection. The excellent electrocatalytic activity of the CuO NWs/GCE may be due to the unique properties of CuO NW electrodes, such as higher surface area and subtle electronic properties. Moreover, the electrocatalytic activity of CuO NWs/GCE was confirmed by conducting CV tests by varying the concentration of PRT (25-150μM) in 0.1M PBS (pH-7.0) at a scan rate of 0.05 $Vs^{-1}$, as shown in Figure (B). The corresponding peak current response vs PRT concentration is shown in Figure (C) shows a linear relationship between PRT concentration and peak current. The redox peak current significantly increases with increase in the PRT concentration (inner to outer: 25-150μM). To examine the detection limit and sensitivity, the CuO NWs/GCE was selected as the working electrode for further investigations, and the oxidation peak was used as the analytical signal in DPV tests because of its higher sensitivity. The electrochemical the oxidation equation of PRT at CuO-NWs/GCE is presented as follows:

$$2Cu^{2+} + C_8H_9NO_2 \rightarrow 2Cu + C_8H_7NO_2 + 2H^+$$

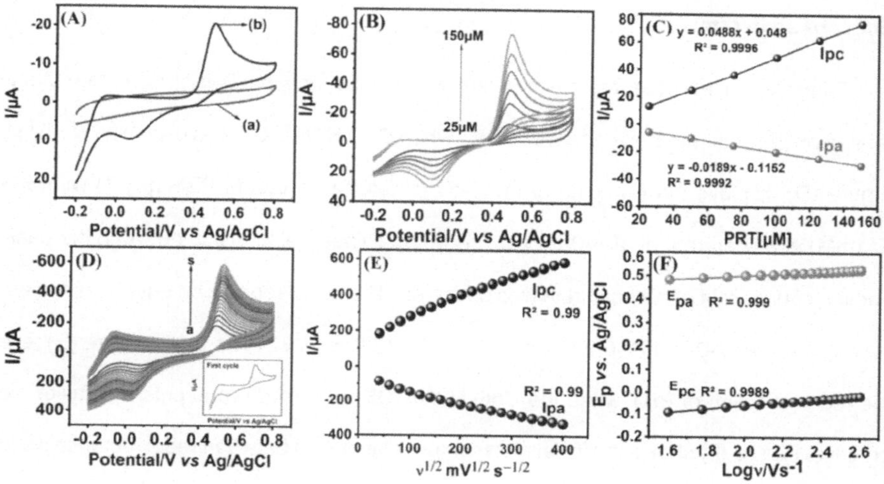


Typical CV curves of electrodes (such as bare GCE (a) and (b) CuO NWs/GCE) (B).CV response of CuO NWs/GCE in the presence of 25-150μM PRT. Supporting electrolyte: PB solution (pH-7.0). (Scan rates $0.05 Vs^{-1}$). The insert was the Current vs concentration relationship

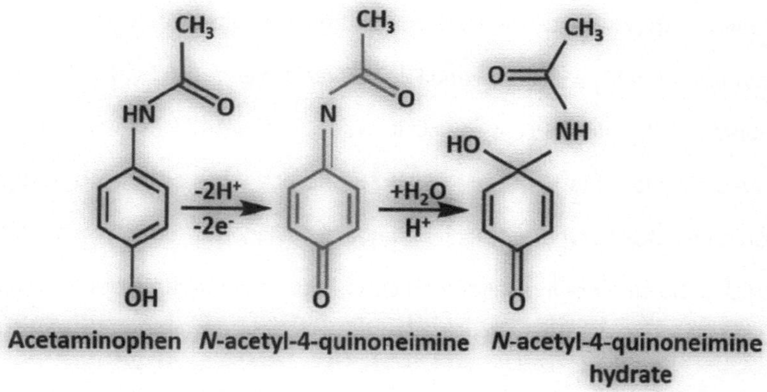


Electrochemical oxidation of PRT on CuO NWs/GCE

### *Effect of scan rate*

To further investigate, the electrochemical oxidation mechanism of PRT, the effect of scan rate (v) on the voltammetry response of PRT when CuO NWs/GCE was used was studied in detail. Figure (D) displays the CV tests of the CuO NWs/GCE in 0.05M PBS (pH 7) with 50μM PRT (0.1mM) at a scan rate of 40-400mV/$s^{-1}$. A notable linear relationship between the peak current and the square root of the scan rate was observed. The linear regression equations are as follows: $I_{pa}$/A=y=−0.0065x-0.794 $R^2$-0.99, and $I_{pc}$/A =y=0.0108x + 1.7274 $R^2$= 0.99. Figure (E) reveals that the redox reaction of PRT when the CuO NWs/GCE was used represents a diffusion-controlled process. Figure (F) shows the Tafel plots for the relationship between redox potential vs log of the different scan rate in seconds.

### *Analytical performance of PRT electrochemical sensor*

Figure (A) displays the DPV curves obtained while using the CuO NWs/GCE for determining PRT. For various concentrations of PRT, a well-defined DPV response was observed. The oxidation peak of PRT increases with the PRT concentration. The plot of the oxidation current versus the PRT concentration suggested good linearity with a linear regression of y=0.0287x + 0.2823 and $R^{2=}$0.99, as presented in Figure (B). The linear range was 100nM to 275.1μM, and the sensitivity was 0.1045 μA/$\mu M^{-1}$ $cm^{-2}$. The limit of detection (LOD) was calculated to be 10 nM (S/N=3). The LOD was calculated using the following equation: LOD=3$S_b$/S, where $S_b$ is the standard deviation of the intercept of the regression line and S is the slope of the calibration curve. Analytical parameters such as linear range and LOD were compared with those in previous studies. The comparison results are presented in Table. In comparison with the electrodes presented in previous studies, the CuO NWs/GCE electrode is the simplest composite with high sensitivity and a wide linear range.

CuO NWs/GCEs are more suitable for future commercialization due to their facile synthesis compared with the electrodes described in previous studies.

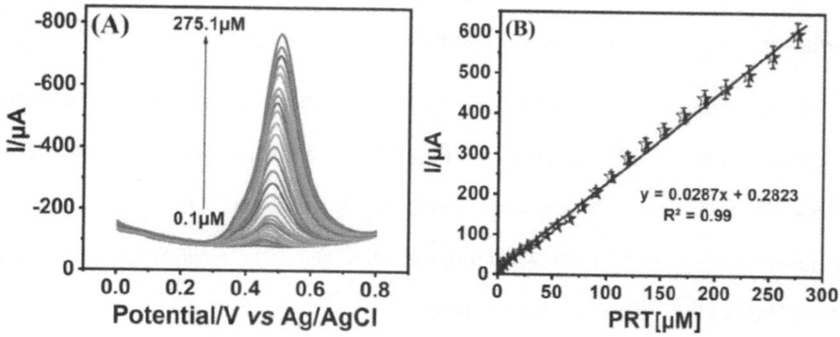


(A). DPVs of paracetamol (from 0.1μM to 275.1μM, at CuO/GCE in 0.05M PBS (pH-7.0)). (B) The plot for peak current vs. paracetamol concentration

**Table-**Comparison of the PRT electrochemical sensors based on CuO NWs/GCE

| Electrodes | Technique | Linear range (μM) | Electrolyte (pH) | LOD (nM) |
|---|---|---|---|---|
| [a]MWCNT/graphene/GCE | DPV | 0.80-110.0 | 7.5 | 90 |
| Graphene/[b]GCE | SWV | 0.1-20 | 9.3 | 32 |
| Boron-doped-diamond electrode | DPV | 0.5-83 | 4.5 | 490 |
| MWCNT/[c]PPGE | SWV | 0.1-25 | 7.5 | 45 |
| Pyrolytic carbon electrode | DPV | 15-225 | 7.0 | 1400 |
| $MoS_2$-[d]GR | DPV | 0.1-100 | 5.5 | 20 |
| MWCNT/chitosan | DPV | 1-145 | 3.0 | 10 |
| Carbon nanotube paste electrode | DPV | 0.15-126 | 7.0 | 43 |
| Carbon-coated-nickel nanoparticles | DPV | 7.8-110 | 5.5 | 2300 |
| Nafion/$TiO_2$-GR/GCE | DPV | 1-100 | 7.0 | 2100 |
| [e]PANI/ MWCNT/GCE | SWV | 1-100 | 5.5 | 2500 |
| CuO [f]NWs/GCE | DPV | 0.1-275.1 | 7.0 | 10 |

[a]MWCNT: multi walled carbon nanotube, [b]GCE: glassy carbon electrode, [c]PPGE: plane pyrolytic graphite electrode, [d]GR: graphene, [e]PANI: poly aniline, [f]NWs: nanowires, [g]LOD: limit of detection, [h]μM: micromole, [i]nM: nanomole.

### *Interference, reproducibility, repeatability, and stability tests*

The repeatability and reproducibility were assessed in the presence of a phosphate buffer (pH 7.0) containing 50μM PRT, as shown in Figure (C and D). The electrode exhibits sustainable repeatability with a relative standard deviation of 1.60% for five repetitive measurements conducted using CuO NWs/GCEs. Moreover, the electrode exhibits good reproducibility of 1.0198% for five independent measurements.

The selectivity performance of the CuO NWs/GCE was analyzed in the presence of some interferences such as dopamine, uric acid, and ascorbic acid, were the results are analyzed. Figure (A) displays the DPV response of the CuO NWs/GCE toward 50μM PRT and 20-fold higher concentration of interfering species (above mentioned). The results revealed that the electrode quickly responded to PRT (Figure (B)) and interfering species. However, very quiet responses were observed when each interfering species were injected separately (without PRT). This suggests excellent selectivity of the electrode.

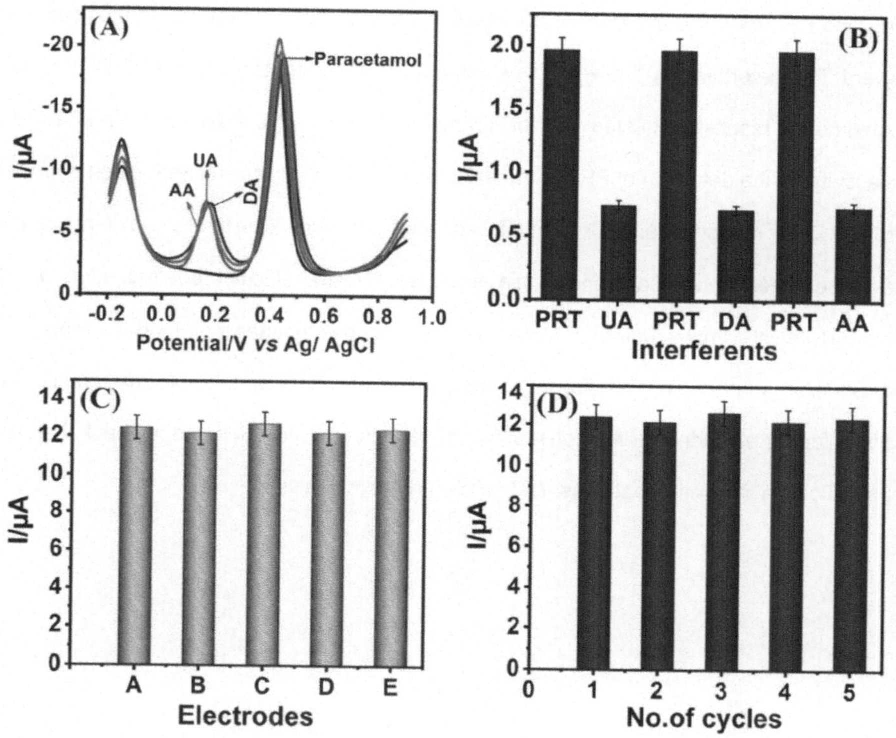


(A) Selectivity for PRT at CuO NWs/GCE in the presence of 0.05M PB solution (pH 7.0). (B) corresponding peak current vs interfering species concentration, (C) Reproducibility of PRT with five different modified electrodes containing 50μM of PRT and (D) Repeatability of the modified electrode with five different cycles of experiment.

***Conclusion***

To summarize the work, we have developed a technolo1gically advanced electrochemical sensor for the effective selection and sensitization, to determine the PRT which was constructed by green synthesis of CuO NW electrodes using a chemical precipitation method. Morphological features of CuO NW electrodes were appropriately characterized structurally using XRD, FTIR,

EIS, and FE-SEM. The excellent electrocatalytic activity enhancement of the modified electrode toward the determination of PRT was confirmed by conducting CV and DPV tests. The experimental results suggested that the prepared electrochemical sensor showed an excellent selectivity for the detection of PRT in the existence of potentially co-interfering compounds with a broader linear response range, lower LOD, and high sensitivity. Due to this excellent behavior, the developed electrochemical sensor can be used for the efficient determination of PRT in pharmaceutical samples in future. Moreover, the proposed synthesis method is simple, fast, and reproducible and does not require any sophisticated instruments. In future, the present process can be further extended for the construction of various morphologies and to check their possible applications in lithium ion batteries, fuel cells, and photocatalysis.

# Chapter-3

## Ultrasonic synthesis of CuO nanoflakes: A robust electrochemical scaffold for the sensitive detection of phenolic hazard in water and pharmaceutical samples

### *Introduction*

Transition metal oxide nanomaterials has gained a considerable attention in the sensor applications due to their distinctive mechanical and electrical features, high photo and electrocatalytic activity, large surface area, cost-effective and excellent stability. Copper oxide (CuO) belongs to the metal oxide nonstoichiometric semiconductor class and having the narrow band gap energy of 1.2 to 1.6 electron volt (eV). Due to the dimensional restraints and morphological structures nano-scale CuO have been widely used than the bulk CuO in various applications such as solar cell panels manufacturing, electrochromic devices, electrocastalysis, photocatalysis, biosensors, gas sensing, field emitters, LIBs, high-tech superconducting materials and methane dissolution from water. Therefore, considering the cost effectiveness, chemical stability, durability, robust and eco-friendly, a lot of efforts have been devoted to develop the CuO nanostructures which including thermal oxidation, ultrasonic irradiation, hydrothermal synthesis, vapor-phase solid preparation, thermal decomposition and electron beam lithography. However, tedious synthesis procedure, usage of hazardous chemicals and surfactants makes them bitter disadvantageous in real time applications. In recent years, the nanomaterials have been successfully synthesized by ultra-sonication method. Compared to the conventional methods, ultrasound-assisted method is simple, eco- and environmental- friendly, which makes their utility to develop the metal oxides with controlled shape, size, phase purity and uniform size distribution. Moreover, the nanomaterials prepared from the ultrasonic assisted synthesis have higher surface area with faster reaction time. Thus, we have developed a surfactant-free, short-term one-step precipitation method followed by ultrasonic irradiation for the synthesis of CuO nanoflakes (CuO-NFs) within 60min with uniform morphology. The synthesized CuO-NFs fabricated sensor will be expected to overcome the aforementioned disadvantages and fulfill the real time applications.

Hydroquinone (1,4-Benzenediol) (HQ) is a white crystalline phenolic compound and a major dihydroxybenzene isomer. It is extensively used to formulate the beauty aids, dye intermediate, as a stabilizer in varnishes, paints, oils and motor fuels, pesticides, antioxidants in rubber and food industry, photographic film developing and added to other industrial monomers to exhibit polymerization during shipping, storage and chemicals processing. Due to the utilization of HQ, water pollution tragedies frequently found by the improper handling and accidental outflows. To date, HQ is listed as a minacious air pollutant according to the clean air act 1990, requiring the environmental protection agency (U.S. EPA) to set emission standards. When HQ is adsorbed directly through the skin, it creates toxic effects to several organs such as kidney, liver, lungs and urinary tract in the living organisms. Aforementioned, about the hazardous effects, we need remarkable selective and sensitive approaches for the quantification of HQ. Currently, a variety of analytical approaches were established for HQ quantification, consisting of high-performance liquid chromatography (HPLC), capillary electrophoresis, spectrophotometry, fluorescence, chemiluminescence, gas chromatography-mass spectroscopy (GC-MS) and some electroanalysis methods. However, most of the analytical techniques, especially chromatographic methods need a complicated experimental set up, sample pretreatment and large amount of organic solvents besides the expensive instruments and prolonged analysis time, make them tedious in practicability. Electroanalytical techniques overcome these barriers for HQ assay and are inexpensive, quick response, high accuracy, excellent sensitivity, good reliability and no need of expensive instrumentations, and hence it became a beneficial approach for industrial and environmental investigations. The non-devastating nature and extremely small quantity of chemical consumption make them one of the preferred techniques. Moreover, since HQ is an electroactive substance, the electroanalytical approaches can be appraised as suitable strong substitute to the previously mentioned techniques.

In the present work, we have developed the short-term one-step precipitation synthesis of CuO-NFs within 60 min reaction time and successfully employed for the sensitive detection of the environmental hazardous pollutant HQ. The formed CuO-NFs were confirmed by XRD, FE- SEM, FT-IR spectroscopy and UV-visible spectroscopy and modified on the screen-printed carbon electrode (SPCE). The SEM images exhibited the uniform CuO-NFs with the average width of 85nm. The linker-free CuO-NFs fabricated electrode was successfully utilized for the determination of HQ. The fabricated sensor having long term stability and sensitivity was exploited for the environmental and commercial real sample analysis, implying that the SPCE/CuO-NFs is an economically viable and benign robust scaffold for HQ determination.

### *Experimental techniques and chemicals*

All the chemicals were of analytical substances and were used without any further purification. Copper sulfate pentahydrate ($CuSO_4.5H_2O$), ammonium hydroxide ($NH_4OH$, 25%) ethanol (75%), hydroquinone, glucose, para-aminophenol, para-nitrophenol, catechol, hydrogen peroxide, hydrazine, chloramphenicol, dibasic sodium phosphate ($Na_2HPO_4$), monobasic sodium phosphate ($NaH_2PO_4$), were received from Sigma-Aldrich. Supporting electrolyte (phosphate buffer (PB) solution; 0.1M, pH-7.0) was prepared using the mixture of $Na_2HPO_4.2H_2O$ and $NaH_2PO_4$ in doubly distilled water (DDW). The pharmaceutical tablet hydroquinone was obtained from the nearby pharmacy in India.

The FT-IR spectra were recorded with the samples on KBR in the Nicolet-410 FT-IR spectrophotometer. The morphological properties of CuO-NFs were characterized by field emission scanning electron microscope (JSM- 6390LV (Jeol, Japan)) attached with energy dispersive X-ray detector. The XRD analysis was carried out at Rigaku X-ray diffractometer with Cu-Ka radiation ($\lambda$=0.154nm) at 30 kV and 15 mA. The optical properties and energy band gap of CuO-NFs were analyzed by UV-vis-DRS spectrophotometer and the band gap energy was calculated from the Tauc plot. The impedance studies were monitored by (EIM6ex Zahner, Germany). All the electrochemical studies were conducted in CH instrument (CHI1205A) in which screen-printed carbon electrode as working, Ag/AgCl as reference and Pt wire employed as counter electrodes. All the potentials mentioned in the figures all are respective to Ag/AgCl reference electrode.

***Preparation of CuO-NFs***

To synthesize CuO-NFs, about 1.0g of $CuSO_4.5H_2O$ was dissolved in 50 ml water and transferred into a RB flask. Then, 25% of 10ml NaOH were added to the above solution at 120ºC under magnetic stirring (800rpm). Afterwards, 0.1g of L-ascorbic acid were added drop wise to the solution and the reaction mixture was ultrasonicated for 2h (irradiation power 100W, 20 kHz). Finally, the as-prepared CuO-NFs was filtered using 0.2μM Whattmann filter paper and successively washed with DDW until the reach of pH 6.5 to 7.0. The product was placed under vacuum for 24 h at 60ºC to obtain the yellow colored solid. Scheme depicts the illustration of CuO-NFs formation and the chemical reaction is,

$$CuSO_4\,(aq) + NaOH\,(aq) \rightarrow Cu\,(OH)_2\,(s) + Na_2SO_4\,(aq) \rightarrow \textbf{(1)}$$

$$Cu\,(OH)_2\,(s) \rightarrow CuO\,(s) + H_2O \rightarrow \textbf{(2)}$$

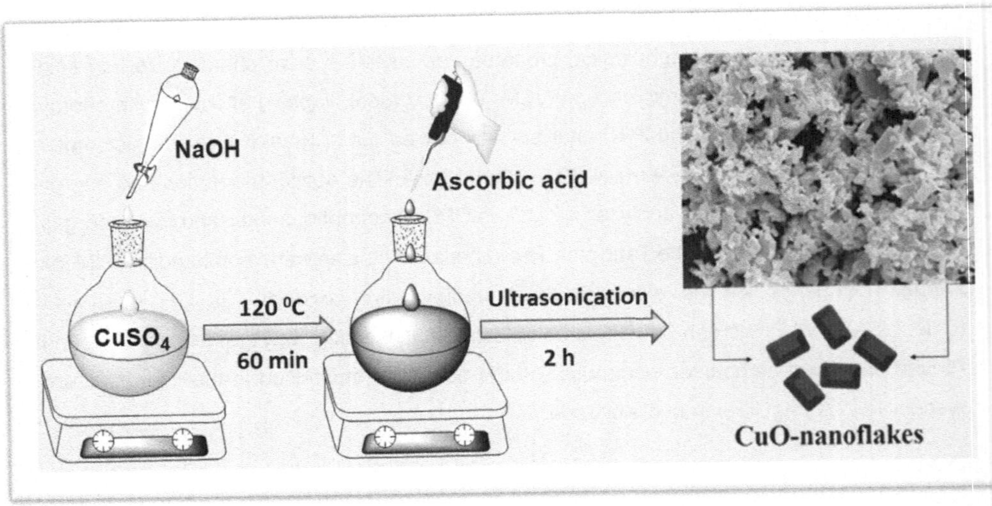


Illustration on the preparation of CuO nanoflakes

***Fabrication of CuO-NFs on SPC electrode***

To prepare the HQ sensor, about 5mg of CuO-NFs were dispersed into the 0.5mL of DDW and allowed to ultrasonication for 30min at room temperature. Afterwards, 20μL CuO-NFs suspension was casted on single core-SPCE surface and dried at 50ºC in a hot air oven for 10min.

**Data collection and interpretation**

To examine the crystalline nature, phase purity and chemical properties of as prepared CuO-NFs, XRD measurements were carried out and depicted in Figure. The CuO-NFs XRD pattern displays the diffraction peaks at 32.44, 35.48, 38.68, 44.73, 48.75, 53.42 and 58.26° correspond to the (1 1 0) (1 1 1), (0 2 2), (1 1 1), (1 5 0), (0 2 0), and (1 1 3) planes of monoclinic CuO, and it is well consistent with JCPDS 48-1548 [38]. No other characteristic peaks of slurvians like $Cu(OH)_2$ or precursors were observed, indicating the formation of pure monoclinic phase of CuO-NFs. The crystallite size of the NFs was calculated by Scherer's formula (eqn 3) by employing the full-width half maximum (FWHM) of a prominent diffraction peak.

$$X_s = k\lambda / \beta \cos\theta \rightarrow (3)$$

where, $X_s$ is denoted the crystallite size, λ generally called X-ray wavelength, ß is the FWHM of the diffraction peak, θ is the angle of Bragg diffraction, and k is Scherer's constant. The crystallite size was calculated for the diffraction plane (111), and the average size was found to be 20.21nm.

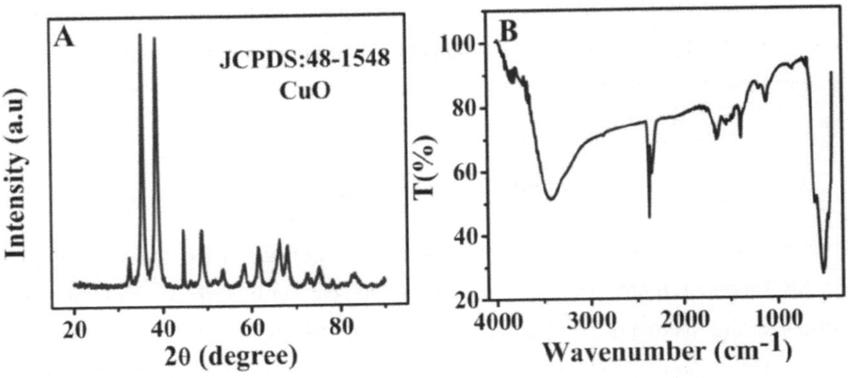


(A) XRD pattern and (B) FT-IR spectrum of CuO-NFs

The FT-IR spectroscopy was employed for the further investigation on the CuO-NFs formation. As seen in Figure, the absorption peaks spectrum at low frequencies below 700cm$^{-1}$ are correlated to the metal-oxide vibrations of monoclinic structure of CuO, while bands at 3415 cm$^{-1}$ correspond to the hydroxyl groups. The broad centered at 1626cm$^{-1}$ were accredit to O-H stretching and bending modes of water. The weak bands around 1380cm$^{-1}$ corresponded to the C-H vibration and the absorption peak at 1114cm$^{-1}$ can be assigned to C-O vibration coordinating to metal anions.

***UV-vis band gap analysis***

The optical properties of CuO-NFs were analyzed from the UV-vis absorption spectral data. As seen in Figure, CuO-NFs shows the absorption band at 265.83nm (Figure A), which are assigned to n-π* transitions. From this absorption data, the band gap energy of CuO were calculated. The optical energy band gap was determined from the Tauc's plot (Figure B). The following equation is used for the estimation of optical band gap energy,

$$\alpha_o h\nu = A\,(h\nu - E_g)^{1/2} \rightarrow (4)$$

Where, A is proportionality constant, ν is the photon's frequency, $\alpha_o$ is the weak-field absorption coefficient, $E_g$ is the optical energy band gap and h is the plank's constant. By plotting $(\alpha_o hv)^2$ versus hv, the average band gap energy of CuO-NFs was estimated and the band gap value has been calculated to be 2.27eV and thus the CuO-NFs is well known to behave as direct band gap semiconductor.

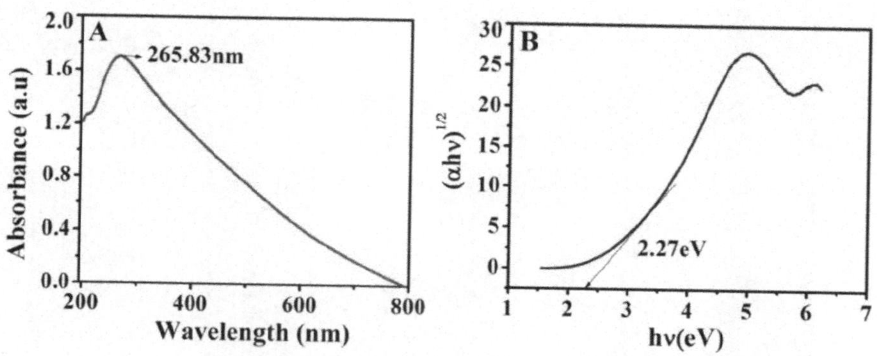


(A) UV-visible spectrum and (B) Tauc's plot of CuO-NFs

***Morphological analysis of CuO-NFs***

The surface morphology of the synthesized CuO-NFs was studied with the aid of FE-SEM attached with an energy dispersive X-ray detector. The images recorded at different magnifications were shown in Figure. The low magnification images displayed the granules of CuO with uniform morphology (Figure A and B) while the higher magnifications exactly revealed the nanoflakes morphology (Figure C and D) with isotropic and uniform structures and the average width of the CuO-NFs was found to be 85 nm. Simultaneously, EDS measurement for CuO-NFs was conducted at 10 keV and shown in (Figure A). It clearly presented the existence of copper (%Cu) and an oxygen (%O) elements in the synthesized CuO nanoflakes with the indication of the merely stoichiometric formation of the CuO-NFs. The elemental mapping analysis justifies the exact location of the Cu and O elements (Figure B-D).

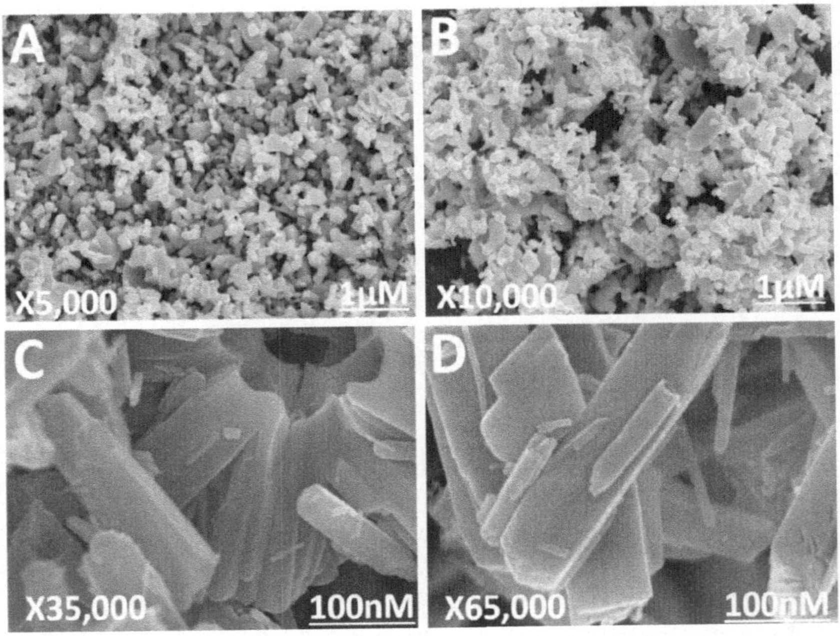


FE-SEM images of CuO-NFs with different magnifications

EDX and elemental mapping profiles of the CuO-NFs

***Electrochemical Impedance Spectral (EIS) analysis***

EIS is an useful tool for monitoring the electrode-electrolyte interface changes and the electrode kinetics arising from the identification events at surface modifications. An electron transfer probe KCl(0.1M )/[$Fe(CN)_6{}^{3-/4-}$](5mM) was utilized to study the electro- kinetics and the obtained EIS results were fitted best with the Randle circuit (Rs[$C_{dl}$-$R_{ct}$-W]) (Figure, inset), where the solution resistance ($R_s$) is in sequel connection with charge transfer resistance ($R_{ct}$) and Warburg resistance (W) and is parallel to the double-layer capacitance ($C_{dl}$). The semicircle diameter of the Nyquist plot reveals the charge transfer kinetics of electrode- electrolyte interface. From Figure, the bare SPCE (curve a) exhibits higher $R_{ct}$ value with negligible electron transfer rate due to low conductance of SPCE. Howbeit, after the fabrication of CuO-NFs (curve b), the Nyquist semicircle portion evolve into a smaller which may be due to high conductivity of CuO-NFs, which enhances the easier electron transfer rate and indicates the lower impedance. The semicircle obtained for the CuO-NFs/SPCE was 10-fold higher than that of the bare SPCE and the $R_{ct}$ values were found to be 1181.61Ω for bare SPCE and 71.14Ω for CuO-NFs/SPCE. The highly conductive CuO-NFs modified electrode drastically reduced the electrical resistivity and hence the much lower $R_{ct}$ value was obtained for the CuO-NFs modified SPCE. These results suggest that the successfully fabricated highly conductive CuO-NFs breaks the resistance barrier between the redox probe and SPCE.

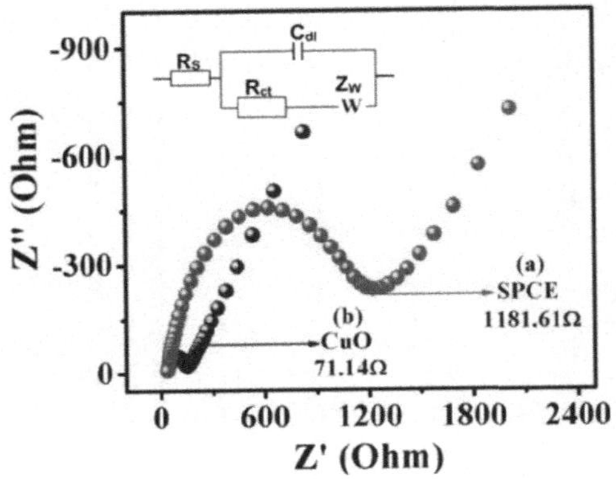


Nyquist semicircle plots of (a) SPCE and (b) CuO-NFs/SPCE in the mixture of 5mM $[Fe(CN)_6]^{3-/4-}$ and 0.1M KCl at ± 5mV amplitude with 0.01-100 kHz frequency range (inset: Randel's equivalent circuit model)

***Electrocatalytic properties of the modified sensor***

Further, the electrochemical features of the constructed sensor were analyzed by cyclic voltammogram (CV) obtained in 0.1M PB solution (pH 7.0) in the potential range of -0.2 to +0.6V at a sweep rate of 0.05V/s. As shown in Figure A, in absence of HQ the bare and modified electrode didn't show any obvious redox peak current, indicating the electrochemical inactivity at the said potential window (curves a and b). Nevertheless, when the CV was conducted at the bare SPCE in the presence of 200μM HQ, a wide quasi-redox peak with peak potential of about +0.26V and +0.003V was observed due to the electrochemical redox behavior of HQ (curve c). Interestingly, the CuO-NFs modified with the SPCE was measured in the presence of same addition of HQ, exhibited a well-shaped quasi-redox peak potentiated at +0.41V and +0.09V (curve d). The highly conducting CuO-NFs increases the electrocatalytic activity by increasing the redox currents of HQ. The electro-redox mechanism of HQ sensor schematically is illustrated in Scheme. During the electrocatalytic reaction, hydroquinone was oxidized and produce $H_2O_2$ and consume $O_2$. Further, the produced $H_2O_2$ generates the electron flow upon oxidation at the CuO-NFs/SPCE and amplify the current response in the addition of different concentrations of HQ from 50 to 300μM (Figure B). The amplified response current can be ascribed the CuO-NFs with high aspect ratio, which contribute a huge specific surface area and excellent electrical conductivity. The over-all electrode mechanism of HQ by CuO-NFs is written as follows (equation),

$$2Cu^{2+} + QH_1 \rightarrow 2Cu + BQ + 2H^+$$

Where, $QH_1$ and BQ denote the HQ and benzoquinone, respectively. The rate of this chemical reaction has been measured as a function of the concentration of HQ and the product. The mechanism involves the ionization of $QH_1$ to $QH^-$, followed by an electron transfer between $QH^-$ and $Cu^{2+}$, reaction equation.

$$Cu^{2+} + QH \leftrightarrows Cu + QH$$

Where, QH denotes the semi-Quinone.

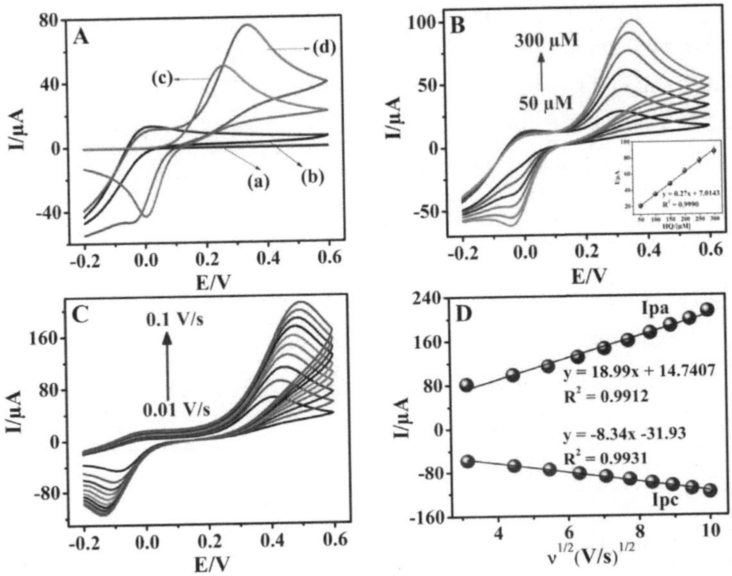


(A) CVs obtained in the (a and b) absence and (c and d) presence of 200µM HQ at (a and c) bare SPCE and (b and d) CuO-NFs/SPCE and (B) at different HQ concentrations from 50-300µM at CuO-NFs/SPCE at 50mV/s. (C) CVs of responses of 200µM HQ at CuO-NFs/SPCE at different sweep rates and (D) plots of the redox currents of HQ vs. square root of scan rate.

***Information from the potential sweep rate***

To better understand the electrochemical HQ response at the CuO-NFs modified electrode, the effect of the sweep rate on the electro-redox peak currents of HQ was analyzed by CV at different sweep rates of 0.01 to $0.1Vs^{-1}$ and shown in Figure C. A parallel of well-defined redox peaks were obtained at the CuO-NFs/SPCE in the window of -0.2 to +0.7V. While increasing the sweep rates, the redox peak currents ($I_{pa}$) and ($I_{pc}$) increased with the increase of the peak separation ($\Delta E_p$). The anodic ($I_{pa}$) and cathodic peak currents ($I_{pc}$) of HQ at the CuO- NFs/SPCE were in linear proportion with the square root of the sweep rates (Figure D.), and linear regression equations are expressed. The above results suggest that the electrochemical process of HQ is controlled by diffusion at the CuO-NFs/SPCE and the electrode mechanism assert the involvement of each two electrons and protons in this electrochemical reaction.

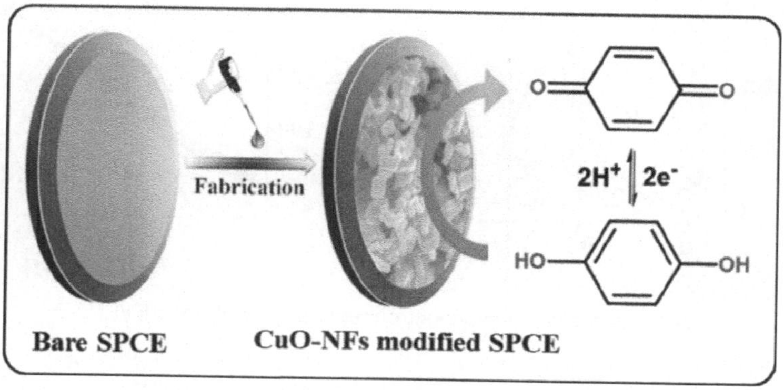


The electro-redox mechanism of HQ at CuO-NFs/SPCE

***Analytical features of HQ electrochemical sensor***

The differential pulse voltammogram (DPV) response of the fabricated CuO-NFs/SPCE is analyzed to evaluate the HQ sensor by adding various HQ concentrations and shown in Figure A and its corresponding calibration curve in Figure B. The modified electrode showed an excellent DPV response upon various HQ level. As shown in Figure A, a clear steady current increase is evident with the increase of HQ concentration from 0.1 to 1400μM. It can be noticed that the increase in the HQ level increases the response current with a range of 0.1 to 1400μM with the high linear relationship ($R^2$=0.998) (Figure B). The regression equation is: I (μA) =0.3537×μM+0.0187 ($R^2$=0.998). The slope delivers the sensitivity of 3.54 $mAcm^{-2}mM^{-1}$, which is the highest value when compared to other reported HQ sensors (Table) and the limit of detection (LOD) was estimated to be 10.4nM (S/N=3) for the fabricated sensor. The higher sensing performance of the CuO-NFs/SPCE can be assigned to the high surface area due to high aspect ratio with high electrical conductivity, which offers an auspicious microenvironment for HQ detection and the direct electron transfer leads the higher-sensitivity, quick response and low- level detection.

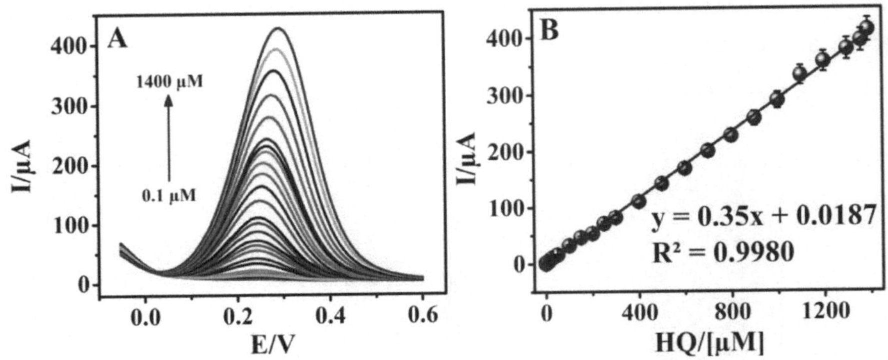


DPVs response of HQ electrochemical sensor on CuO/SPCE

The specificity of the CuO-NFs/SPCE towards HQ detection in several possible co-interfering species medium is investigated by DPV measurements. As shown in Figure A, the CuO-NFs/SPCE shows well-defined DPV current response for each addition of 50 µM of HQ, at the same time, there is no noteworthy peak current was observed in the presence of 50-fold excess concentration of biologically co-interfering chemicals, pharmaceuticals, organic and inorganic substances such as, para-aminophenol (4-AP), para-nitrophenol (4-NP), hydrazine (HZ), catechol (CC), chloramphenicol (CAP), cadmium (Cd2+), lead (Pb2+), sulphate (SO4 2-), hydrogen peroxide (HP) and glucose (Glu). Since CC is structurally isomeric with HQ, it affects the response current of HQ slightly. The DPV responses of HQ in the co-existence of the aforesaid interfering agents, suggesting that the developed sensor possessed an excellent specificity and the corresponding response current chart is as seen in the Figure B. The above results strongly demonstrate that the as-prepared HQ sensing platform of CuO-NFs will perform well for future environmental applications.

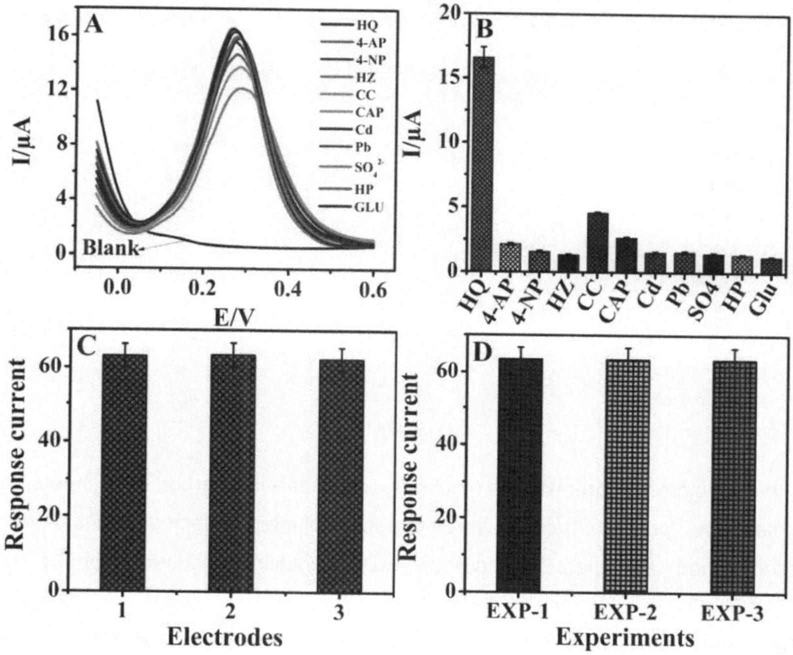


(A) DPVs obtained for each 50μM addition of HQ in the presence of various environmental and biological interferences at CuO-NFs/SPCE and (B) its corresponding current response plot. (C) Repeatability (D) reproducibility of the CuO-NFs/SPCE electrode towards HQ

The repeatability and reproducibility of the proposed sensor were conducted in three independently fabricated SPCEs by CVs with 50μM HQ. It satisfactorily exhibits a good reproducibility with 1.3% relative standard deviation (RSD). Further, the present sensor delivered a tolerable repeatability with 1.5% RSD for 3 consecutive measurements in a set of three different modified electrodes in 50μM HQ in 0.1M PB solution (pH 7) (Figure C-D), indicating the excellent reproducibility and repeatability of the proposed sensor towards the determination of HQ.

Comparison of the CuO-NFs/SPCE HQ sensor with various reported sensors

| Modified electrodes | Technique | Linear range (μM) | Detection limit (μM) | pH & Buffer |
|---|---|---|---|---|
| aPNA/Cd-ZnWO$_4$/bCPE | DPV | 1-56 | 0.17 | 7.0- PBS |
| cGCNS/dGCE | DPV | 0.1-30 | 0.02 | 7.0- PBS |
| ePNR/CPE | DPV | 20-120 | 4.9 | 7.0- PBS |
| f3DIPC-700/GCE | DPV | 0.06-30 | 0.021 | 6.0 – PBS |
| AgNP/gMWCNT/GCE | SWV | 2.5-260 | 0.16 | 3.0 – PBS |
| ZnS/NiS@ZnS | DPV | 0.1-300 | 0.024 | 7.5 – PBS |
| AuNPs-hMPS/CPE | DPV | 10-1000 | 1.2 | 7.0 – PBS |
| Poly(niacinamide)/CPE | CV | 10-160 | 0.24 | 7.4 – PBS |
| NiO/MWCNT/GCE | DPV | 7.4-56 | 0.039 | 6.0 – PBS |
| iPANi–Fe$_2$O$_3$–jrGO | DPV | 0.1–550 | 0.06 | 2.5 – PBS |
| CuO-nanoflakes/SPCE | DPV | 0.1-1400 | 0.0104 | 7.0-PBS |

[a]poly-(nicotinic acid), [b]carbon paste electrode, [c]graphene-like carbon nanosheets, [d]glassy carbon electrode, [e]poly (neutral red), [f]three-dimensional interconnected porous carbon, [g]multi walled carbon nanotubes, [h]mesoporous silica, [i]polyaniline, [j]reduced graphene oxide.

The storage stability is another important criterion for the newly fabricated HQ sensor. The stability of the CuO-NFs/SPCE was analyzed by CV using the 40 days old CuONFs/ SPCE, which is stored in 0.1M PBS. This electrode retained 97.5% of its early response current after 40 days, suggesting that the CuO-NFs/SPCE had substantial storage stability of the sensing.

***Real sample analysis***

To evaluate the practical application of the CuO-NFs modified electrode, an attempt was made to detect the HQ in the water and pharmaceutical samples. These samples are obtained from the nearest river, municipal sewage, and pharmacy. Each sample was diluted with 0.1M PBS (pH-7.0), before measurement in DPV and spiked with different concentrations of HQ except in the pharmaceuticals. The obtained analytical results were tabulated and shown good recovery in the range of 98-99% for HQ. These results indicated that CuO-NFs/SPCE could produce results accurate enough for environmental diagnosis and will be an environmentally benign, economically viable robust scaffold for the determination of environmental pollutants.

Practical application of modified electrode in environmental samples

| Samples | Added (μM) | Found (μM) | Recovery (%) | RSDa (%) |
|---|---|---|---|---|
| River water | 20 | 19.68 | 98.40 | 1.34 |
| Sewage water | 20 | 19.44 | 97.20 | 1.13 |
| Drinking water | 20 | 19.93 | 99.65 | 1.13 |
| Hydroquinone tablet | - | 3.08 | - | 1.18 |
| | 20 | 23.10 | 115.5 | 1.20 |

a-relative standard deviation

### *Conclusion*

In conclusion, an ultrasonic synthesis method was developed for the synthesis of CuO-nanoflakes for the first time and utilized for the electrochemical sensing of the phenolic environmental pollutant HQ. The optical and band gap of CuO-NFs has been investigated and it was found to be 2.27eV. The synthesized CuO-NFs were fabricated on SPCE without the aid of any linker and the fabricated sensor exhibited an excellent selectivity, reliability, stability and durability. The as-prepared sensor exhibited the lowest-detection limit of 10.4nM with the excellent sensitivity of 3.54 $mAcm^{-2}mM^{-1}$. The obtained long-time stabilization of this proposed sensor has 40 days when compared with previously published reports. The fabricated CuO-NFs/SPCE will be a certain useful tool in the diverse Opto-electro chemical devices and also an ideal material for the determination environmental pollutants.

# Chapter-4

## Synthesis of silver phosphate modified copper oxide nanoparticles and their photocatalytic applications

### *Photocatalysis*

Photocatalysis is the acceleration of a photoreaction in the presence of a catalyst. In catalyzed photolysis, light is absorbed by an adsorbed substrate. A catalyst does not change in itself or being consumed in the chemical reaction. This definition includes photosensitization, a process by which a photochemical alteration occurs in one molecular entity as a result of initial absorption of radiation by another molecular entity called the photosensitized. Chlorophyll of plants is a type of photocatalyst. Photocatalysis compared to photosynthesis, in which chlorophyll captures sunlight to turn water and carbon dioxide into oxygen and glucose, photocatalysis creates strong oxidation agent to breakdown any organic matter to carbon dioxide and water in the presence of photocatalyst, light and water. Chlorophyll of plants is a type of photocatalyst. Photocatalysis compared to photosynthesis, in which chlorophyll captures sunlight to turn water and carbon dioxide into oxygen and glucose, photocatalysis creates strong oxidation agent to breakdown any organic matter to carbon dioxide and water in the presence of photocatalyst, light and water as shown in Figure.

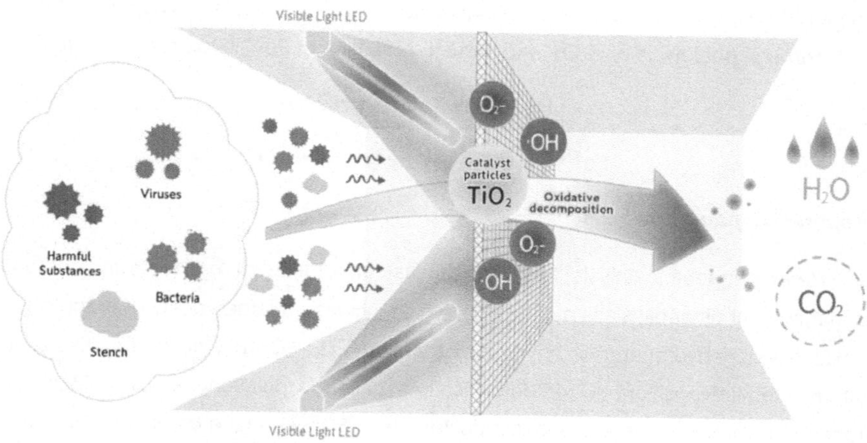


***Homogeneous photocatalysis***

In homogeneous photocatalysis, the reactants and the photocatalyst exist in the same phase. The most commonly used homogeneous photocatalyst include, ozone, transition metal oxide and photo-Fenton systems ($Fe^+$ and $Fe^+/H_2O_2$). The reactive species is the •OH which is used for different purposes. The mechanism of hydroxyl radical production by ozone can follow two paths.

$$O_3 + hv \rightarrow O_2 + O(1D)$$

$$O(1D) + H_2O \rightarrow \bullet OH + \bullet OH$$

$$O(1D) + H_2O \rightarrow H_2O_2$$

$$H_2O_2 + hv \rightarrow \bullet OH + \bullet OH$$

Similarly, the photo-Fenton system produces hydroxyl radicals by the following mechanism.

$$Fe^{2+} + H_2O_2 \rightarrow HO\bullet + Fe^{3+} + OH^-$$

$$Fe^{3+} + H_2O_2 \rightarrow Fe^{2+} + HO\bullet 2 + H^+$$

$$Fe^{2+} + HO\bullet \rightarrow Fe^{3+} + OH^-$$

In photo-Fenton type processes, additional sources of OH radicals should be considered; through photolysis of $H_2O_2$, and through reduction of $Fe^{3+}$ ions under UV light:

$$H_2O_2 + h\nu \rightarrow HO\bullet + HO\bullet$$

$$Fe^{3+} + H_2O + h\nu \rightarrow Fe^{2+} + HO\bullet + H^+$$

***Heterogeneous photocatalysis***

Heterogeneous catalysis has the catalyst in a different phase from the reactants. Heterogeneous photocatalysis is a discipline, which includes a large variety of reactions: mild or total oxidations, dehydrogenation, hydrogen transfer, $^{18}O_2$-$^{16}O_2$ and deuterium-alkane isotopic exchange, metal deposition, water detoxification, gaseous pollutant removal. Most common heterogeneous photocatalyst are semiconductors, which have unique characteristics. Unlike the metals which have a continuum of electronic states, semiconductors possess a void energy region where no energy levels are available to promote recombination of an electron and hole produced by photo activation in the solid. The void region, which extends from the top of the filled valence band to the bottom of the vacant conduction band, is called the band gap. When the semiconductor absorbs a photon with energy equal to or greater than the materials band gap, an electron is excited from the valence band to the conduction band, generating a positive hole in the valence band. The excited electron and hole can recombine and release the energy gained from the excitation of the electron as heat.

***Amaranth***

Amaranth is an anionic dye. It can be applied to natural and synthetic fibers, leather, paper and phenol-formaldehyde resins. As a food additive, it has number E123. Amaranth usually comes as a trisodium salt. It has the appearance of reddish-brown, dark red to purple water-soluble powder that decomposes at 120ºC without melting. Its water solution has absorption maximum at about 520nm.

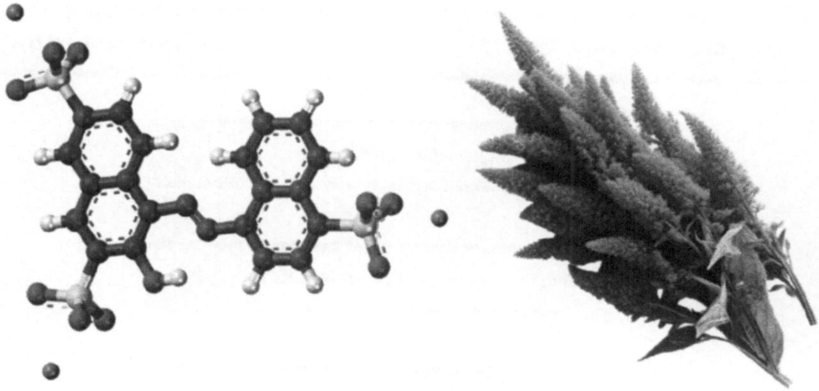

Structure of Amaranth

## Experimental details

### *Synthesis of CuO NPs*

5g of cupric nitrate ($CuNO_3$) dissolved in 100ml double distilled water and sodium hydroxide was added to adjust the pH of the solution with constant stirring for 2hrs. The resulting precipitate was washed several time by using double distilled water and dried over 120°C for 2hrs under hot air oven. It was calcined in a muffle furnace at 500ºC for 1hr.

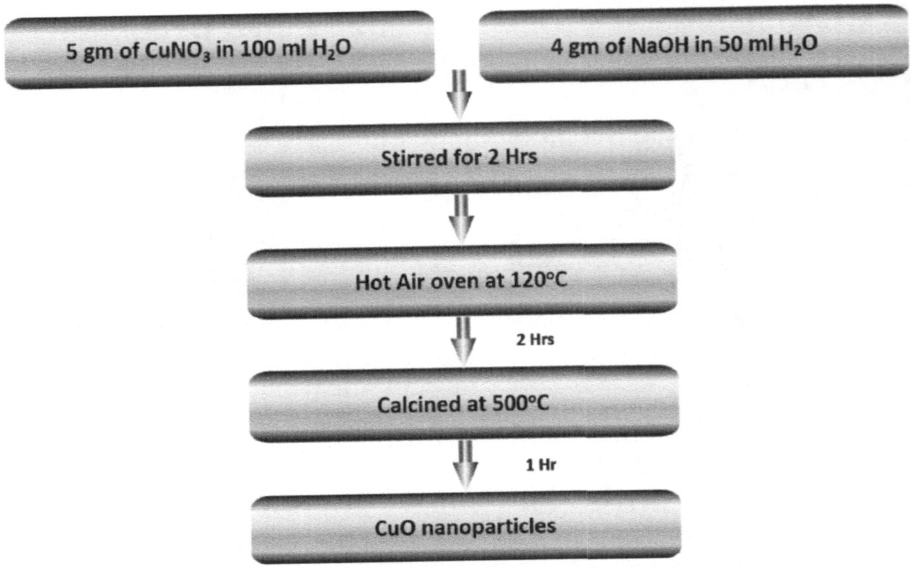


Synthesis of CuO NPs

***Synthesis of $Ag_3PO_4$ NPs***

In a typical synthesis, aqueous citric acid solution (50ml, 0.1M) was introduced dropwise into $AgNO_3$ aqueous solution (50ml, 0.05M) in a beaker, the mixture was stirred for 50min in order to obtain a clear solution. After that aqueous $Na_2HPO_4$ solution (15ml, 0.02M) was added dropwise to the mixture, the reaction mixture was sealed and kept stirring for additional 2hrs. The obtained precipitate was collected by centrifugation, washed several times with absolute ethanol and distilled water and finally dried at 60°C in an air hot oven followed by calcination at 500°C.

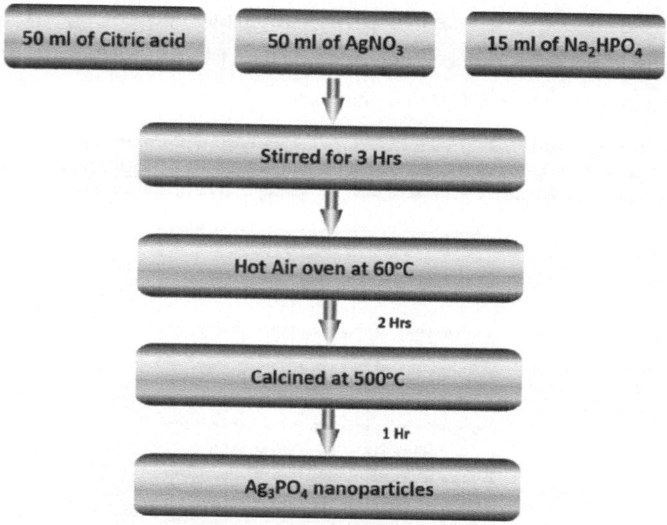


Synthesis of $Ag_3PO_4$

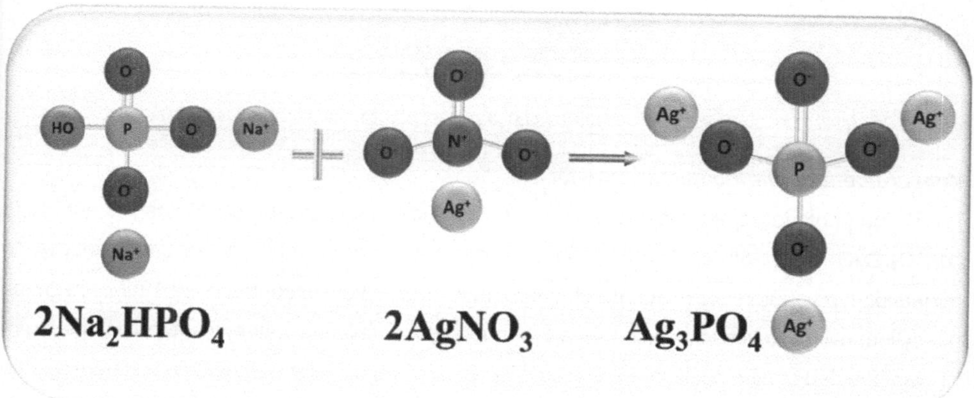


$Ag_3PO_4$ formation mechanism

***Synthesis of $Ag_3PO_4$ doped CuO***

In a typical procedure, 5g of CuO nanoparticles was dispersed in 50ml of ethanol and sonicated for 30min. 1.3142g of $Ag_3PO_4$ was dispersed in 50ml of ethanol and sonicated for 30min.

$Ag_3PO_4$ solution was added drop wise into above CuO solution under magnetic stirring and kept stirring for 1h. The $Ag_3PO_4$/CuO nanocomposites was then filtered, washed and dried in an air hot oven for 120°C and calcined for 500°C in muffle furnace.

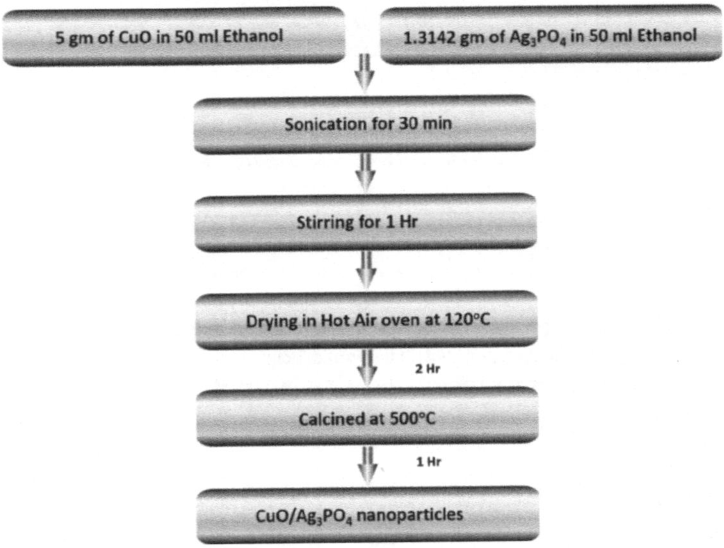


Synthesis of $AgPO_4$/CuO

***Measurement of photocatalytic activity***

The photodegradation of amaranth was adopted to evaluate the photocatalytic activity of $Ag_3PO_4$/CuO in a photoreaction apparatus. Photocatalytic experiments were carried out in an immersion type photoreactor. 300mL of amaranth with an initial concentration of 10µM was taken in a cylindrical glass vessel, which was surrounded by a circulating water jacket to cool the lamp. Air was bubbled continuously into the aliquot by an air bump inorder to provide a constant source of dissolved oxygen. Before light irradiation, the reaction mixture was stirred in dark for 30min to achieve the adsorption-desorption equilibrium between the catalyst and dye molecules. A 300W Xe arc lamp with an ultraviolet cut off filter was used as the visible light irradiation source. During the course of light irradiation, 5mL of aliquot was collected at regular time interval of 30 min. Then the samples were centrifuged to remove the photocatalyst and the filtrate was analyzed by UV-

Visible spectrometer at $\lambda_{max}$=520nm. The photodegradation of Amaranth was calculated by the formula given below:

$$\text{Photodegradation (\%)} = \frac{C_0 - C}{C_0} \text{ X } 100$$

Where, $C_0$ is the concentration of Amaranth before irradiation time and C is the concentration of Amaranth after a certain irradiation time. The schematic representation for the immersion type photoreactor and measurement of photocatalytic activity is shown in Figures.

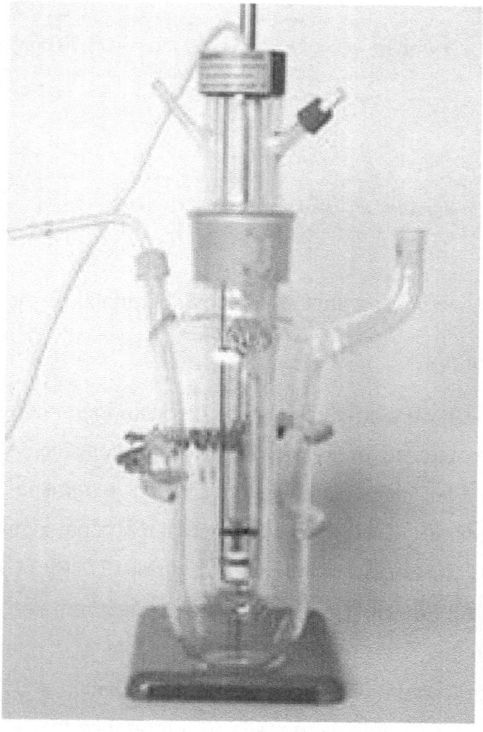

Immersion type photoreactor

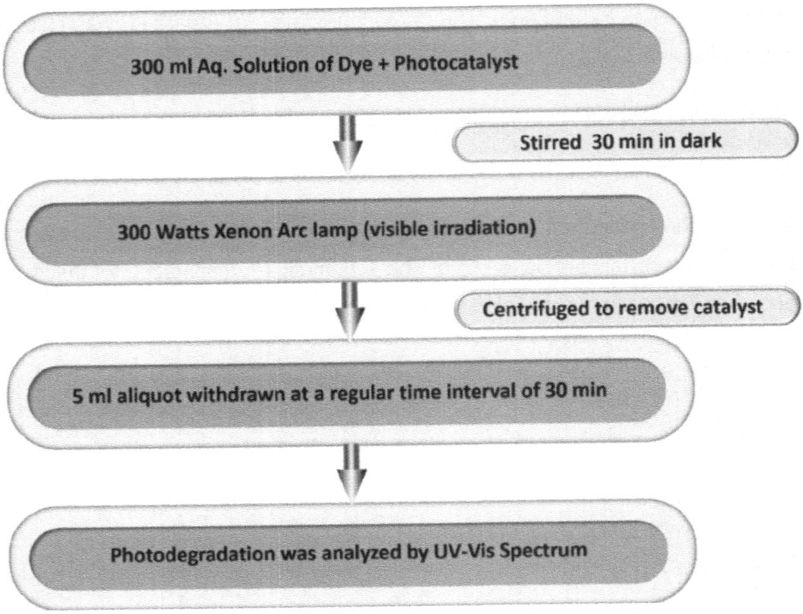


The schematic diagram for the photodegradation of Amaranth dye

***Characterization Technique***

The nanoparticle were characterized by the following methods. The UV-visible diffuse reflectance spectra were obtained for dry-pressed disk sample using JASCO V-550 double beam spectrophotometer with PMT detector equipped with an integrating sphere assembly, using $BaSO_4$ as a reference sample. The spectra were recorded at room temperature ranging from 200 nm to 800nm. Fourier Transformation Infrared Spectrum (FT-IR) of synthesized sample was obtained using Shimadzu Fourier Transform Infrared Spectrometer (IR Affinity-1) with KBr-nanoparticles mixture in the form of pellets. The structure and phase of the samples were determined by X-Ray and powder diffraction with Cu Kα radiation at 25°C using XPERT PRO X-RAY and the structural assignments were made with reference to the standard JCPDS powder diffraction files. Scanning Electron Microscope (SEM) of the nanoparticles were taken by a JM-6701F-6701 instrument in both secondary and backscattered electron modes. The elemental analysis was detected by an energy dispersive X-Ray spectroscopy (EDX) attachment to the SEM.

***X-ray diffraction (XRD)***

Upto 1895 the study of matter at the atomic level was a difficult task but the discovery of electromagnetic radiation with 1Å ($10^{-10}$m) wavelength, appearing at the region between gamma-rays and ultraviolet, makes it possible. As the atomic distance in matter is comparable with the wavelength of X-ray, the phenomenon of diffraction find its way through it and gives many promisable results related to the crystalline structure. The unit cell and lattices which are distributed in a regular three-dimensional way in space forms the base for diffraction pattern to occur. These lattices form a series of parallel planes with its own specific d-spacing and with different orientations exist. The reflection of incident monochromatic X-ray from successive planes of crystal lattices when the difference between the planes is of complete number n of wavelengths leads to famous Brgg's law:

$$n\lambda = 2d\sin\theta$$

Where n is an integer 1, 2, 3....., (Usually equal 1), λ is wavelength in angstroms (1.54A° for copper), d is interatomic spacing in angstroms, and θ is the diffraction angle in degrees. Plotting the angular positions and intensities of the resultant diffracted peaks of radiation produces a pattern, which is a characteristic of the sample. The fingerprint characterization of crystalline materials and the determination of their structure are the two fields where XRD has been mostly used. Unique characteristic x-ray diffraction pattern of each crystalline solid gives the designation of "fingerprint technique" to XRD for its identification. XRD may be used to determine its structure, i.e. how the atoms pack together in the crystalline state and the interatomic distance and angle are etc. From these points it can be concluded that X-ray diffraction has become a very important and powerful tool for the structural characterization in solid state physics and materials science in Figure.

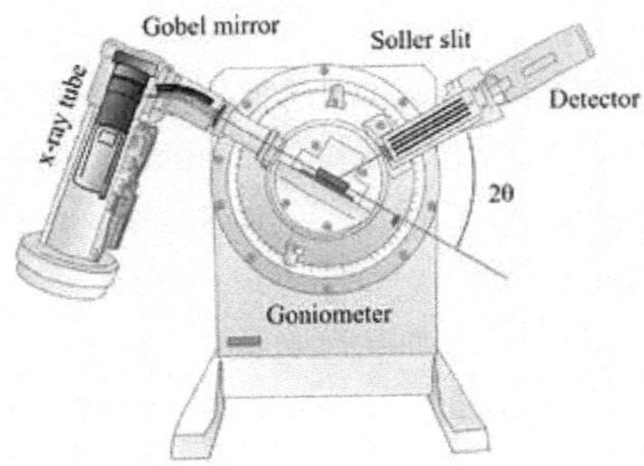
Gobel mirror
Soller slit
x-ray tube
Detector
2θ
Goniometer

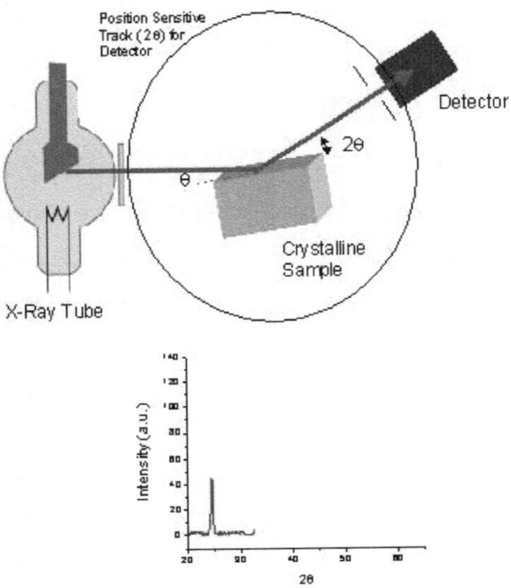
Position Sensitive
Track (2θ) for
Detector
Detector
2θ
θ
Crystalline
Sample
X-Ray Tube
Intensity (a.u.)
2θ

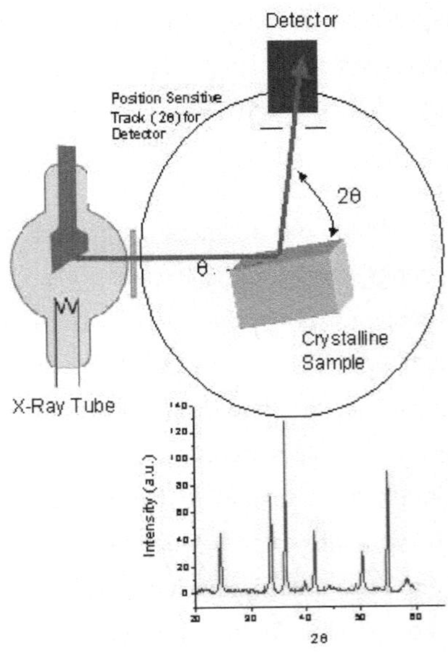
Detector
Position Sensitive
Track (2θ) for
Detector
2θ
θ
Crystalline
Sample
X-Ray Tube
Intensity (a.u.)
2θ

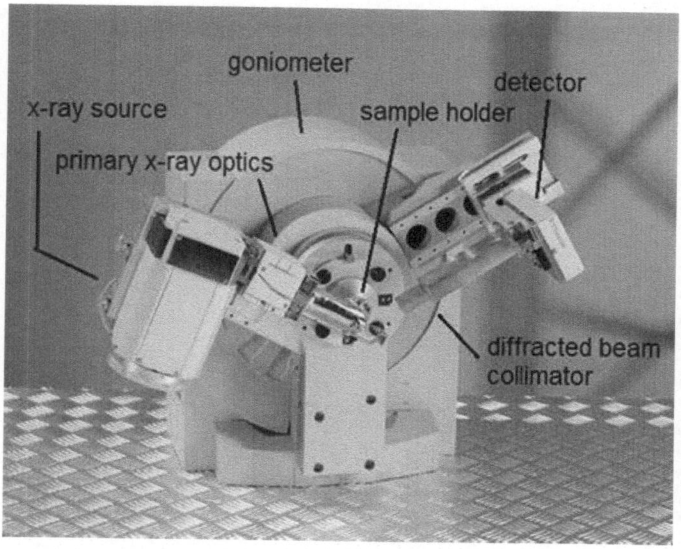


XRD instruments

***Scanning Electron Microscopy (SEM)***

The SEM is a microscope that uses electrons rather than light to form an image. The SEM displays finer morphological details of a specimen surface in Figure .The resolution of SEM is determined by the size of electron beam arriving at the specimen with sufficient current intensity for generating a secondary electron signal of good signal to noise ratio for image formation. The instrument has the following components like electron source, considering lens, scan coil, objective lens, detector amplifier and a monitor. The samples are usually mounted on a double adhesive tape coated with gold in vacuum using a HITACHI HUS-5 vacuum evaporator. If the samples are conducting, they are directly mounted onto sample holder with silver paste. The less-conducting samples are to be gold-sputtered before talking it onto the specimen stage of the SEM. There are many advantages of using the SEM instead of a light microscope. It has a large depth of field, which follows a large amount of the sample to in the focus at one time. The SEM also produces images of high resolution, which means that closely spaced features can be examined at a high magnification.

***SEM operation***

- Air pumped out (vacuum).
- e- gun emits beam of high energy electrons.
- e- beam focused via lenses.
- Scanning coils move beam across sample.
- Secondary electrons are "knocked off "surface.
- Detector counts electrons.
- Image given by $e^-$ Resolution ~5nm.

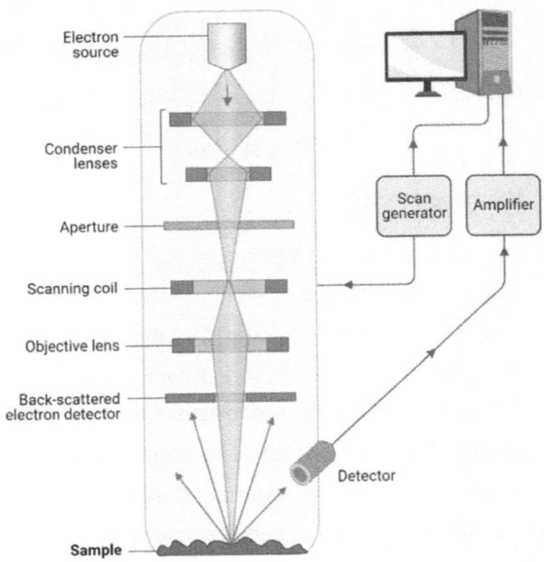

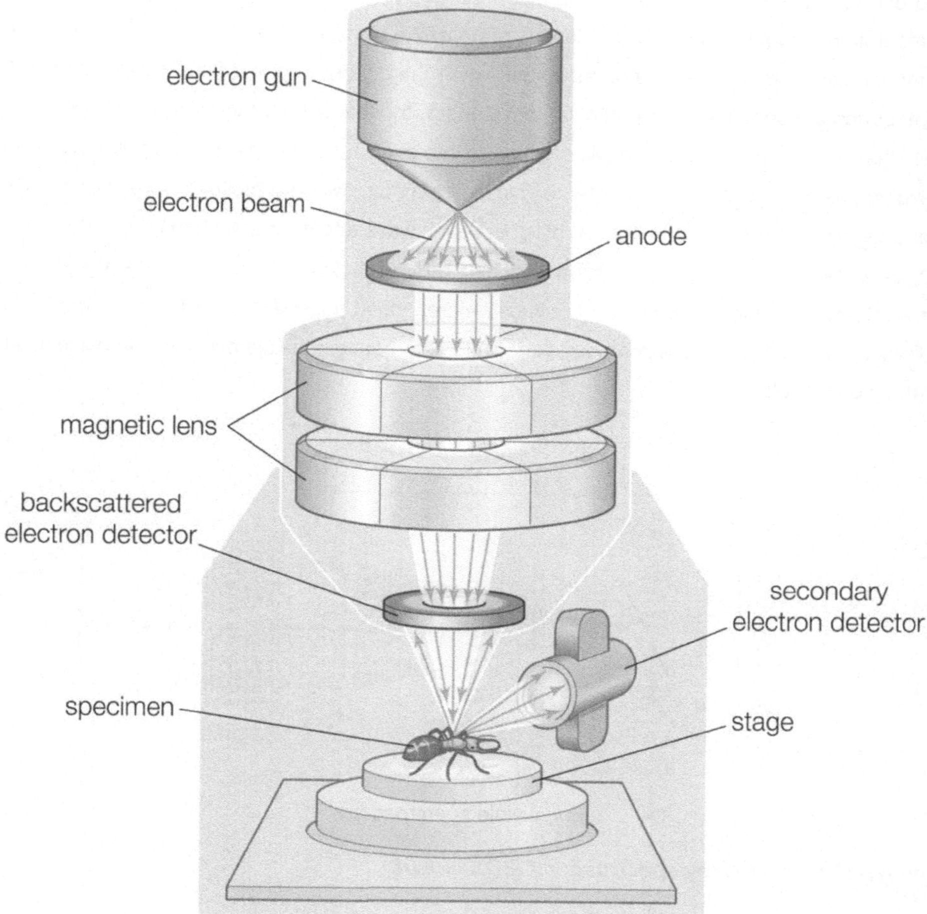


Scanning Electron Microscopy

***UV-Visible spectroscopy***

The wavelength of UV is shorter than the visible light. It ranges from 100 to 400nm. In a standard UV-Vis spectrophotometer, a beam of light is split; one half of the beam (the sample beam) is directed through a transparent cell containing a solution of the compound being analyzed, and one half (the reference beam) is directed through an identical cell that does not contain the compound but contains the solvent. The instrument is designed so that it can make a comparison of the intensities of the two beams as it scans over the desired region of the wavelengths. If the compounds absorbs light at a particular wavelength, the intensity of the sample (Is) will be less than that of the reference beam. Absorption of radiation by a sample is measured at various wavelengths and plotted by a recorder to give the spectrum, which is plot of the wavelength of the entire region versus the absorption (A) of light at each wavelength. And the bandgap of the sample can be obtained by plotting the graph between (αhv vs hv) and extrapolating it along X-axis. Ultraviolet and visible spectrometry is almost entirely used for quantitative analysis, that is, the estimation of the amount of a compound known to be present in the simple. The sample is usually examined in solution.

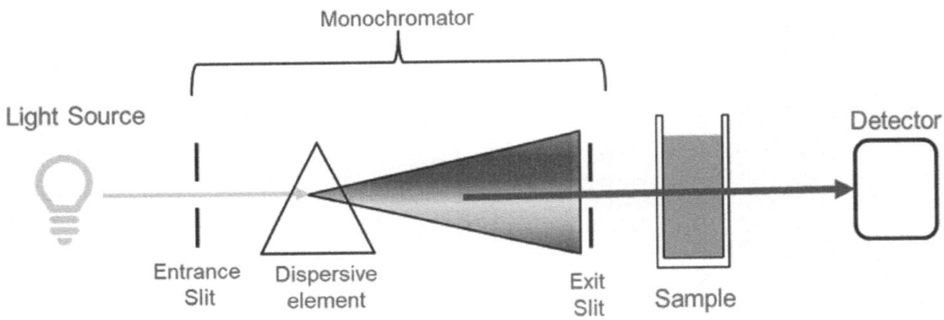


UV-Visible spectroscopy

***Energy dispersive X-ray spectroscopy (EDX or EDS)***

EDX is a chemical microanalysis technique used in conjunction with scanning electron microscopy (SEM). The EDX technique detects X-rays emitted from the sample during bombardment by an electron beam to characterize the elemental composition of the analyzed volume. Features or phases as small as 1µm or less can be analyzed. When the sample is bombarded by the SEM's electron beam, electrons are ejected from the atoms comprising the sample's surface. The resulting electron vacancies are filled by electrons from a higher state, and an X-ray is emitted to balance the energy difference between the two electrons' states. The X-ray energy is characteristic of the element from which it was emitted. The EDX X-ray detector measures the relative abundance of emitted X-rays versus their energy. The detector is typically a lithium-drifted silicon. When an incident X-ray strikes the detector, it creates a charge pulse that is proportional to the energy of the X-ray. The charge pulse is converted to a voltage pulse (which remains proportional to the X-ray energy) by a charge-sensitive preamplifier. The signal is then sent to a multichannel analyzer where the pulses are sorted by voltage. The energy, as determined from the voltage measurement, for each incident X-ray is sent to a computer for display and further data evaluation. The spectrum of X-ray energy versus counts is evaluated to determine the elemental composition of the sampled volume.

***Fourier transform infrared spectroscopy (FTIR)***

In the region of longer wavelength of low frequency, the identification of different type of chemicals is possible by this technique of infrared spectroscopy and the instrument requires for its execution is Fourier transform infrared (FTIR) spectrometer. The spectroscopy merely based on the face that molecules absorb specific frequencies that are characteristic of their structure termed as resonant frequencies i.e. the frequency of the absorbed radiation matches the frequency of the bond or group that vibrates. In addition, the detection of energy is done based on shape of the molecular potential energy surface, the masses of the atoms, and the associated vibronic coupling. Sometimes help of approximation technique like Born -Oppenheimer and harmonic approximation are also taken. As each different material is a unique combination of atoms, no two compounds produce the exact same infrared spectrum. Therefore, infrared spectroscopy can result in a positive identification (qualitative analysis) of every different kind of material. In addition, the size of the peaks in the spectrum is a direct indication of the amount of material present. FTIR can be used to analyze a wide range of materials in bulk or thin films, liquids, solids, pastes, powders, fibers, and other forms. FTIR analysis can give not only qualitative (identification) analysis of materials, but with relevant standards up to ~11 millimeters in diameter, and either measure in bulk or the top ~1 micrometer layer. FTIR spectra of pure compounds are generally so unique that they are like a molecular “fingerprint”.

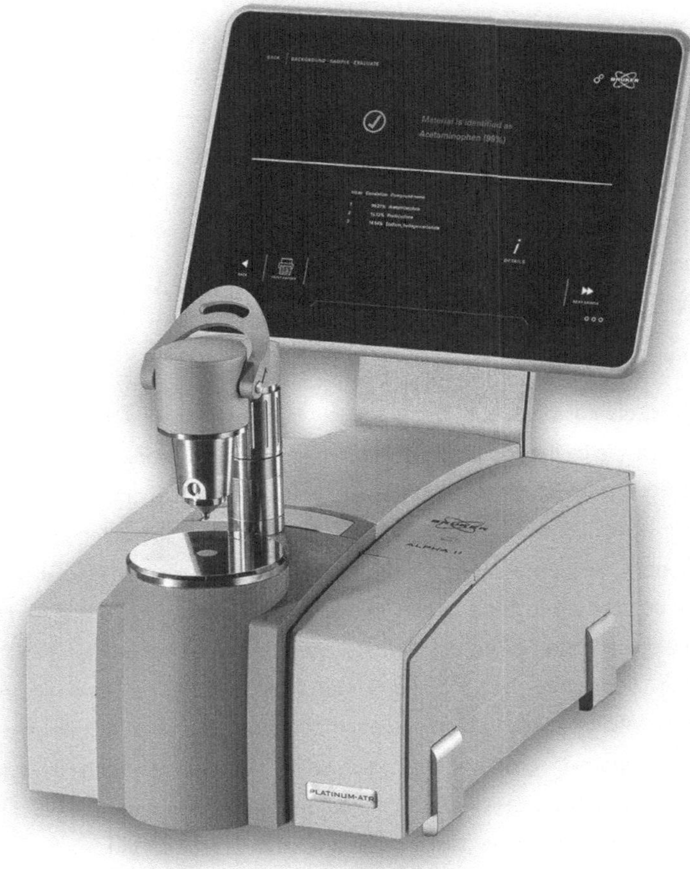


Fourier transform infrared spectroscopy

***Transmission Electron Microscopy (TEM)***

The transmission electron microscopy (TEM) instrument is shown in Figure. In TEM, a thin sample, typically less than 200nm, is bombarded by a highly focused beam of single-energy electrons of very short wavelength, emitted from a tungsten filament at the top of a cylindrical column of about 2m height. The whole optical system of the microscope is enclosed in vacuum. Air must be evacuated from the column to create a vacuum so that the collision of electrons with air molecules and the scattering of electrons are avoided. An image is formed from the interaction of the electrons transmitted through the specimen; the image is magnified and focused onto an imaging device, such as a fluorescent screen, on a layer of photographic film, or to be detected by a sensor such as a CCD (Charge coupled device) camera. Transmission electron diffraction patterns help to determine the crystallographic structure of a material. Amplitude-contrast images yield information about the chemistry and microstructure of a material and its defects. High-resolution (HR) TEM imaging gives information about the microstructure of a material and its defects at an atomic resolution. The possibility for high magnifications has made the TEM a valuable tool in medical, biological and materials research.

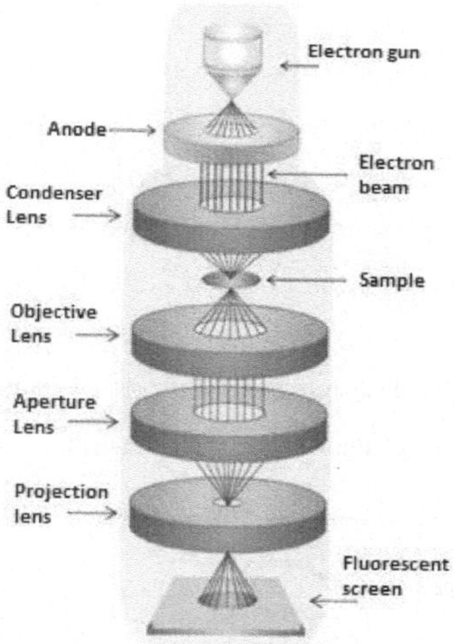


Transmission Electron Microscopy

## Result and Discussion

### *UV-Vis-DRS*

In order to investigate the band gap of CuO, $Ag_3PO_4$ and $Ag_3PO_4/CuO$ nanoparticles, the absorption spectra of synthesized CuO, $Ag_3PO_4$ and $CuO/Ag_3PO_4$ were examined by UV-Vis-DRS spectrophotometer and the results are shown in Figure (a). The pure $Ag_3PO_4$ showed a fundamental absorption edge at about 500nm. The $Ag_3PO_4/CuO$ samples showed enhancing in the visible region and the visible absorption intensity of the photocatalyst were increased with the increasing CuO content because CuO was the good light absorptive material, the similar result has been reported by Yu. Meanwhile, it was observed that the color composite sample became darker (from yellow to dark yellow) when more and more black CuO were introduced into the pure $Ag_3PO_4$ nanoparticles. This result indicated that the photocatalyst could absorb more photons. Therefore, it might be favorable for photocatalytic reaction. The band gap was calculated by Tauc's formula which shows the relationship among coefficient and the incident photon energy of $Ag_3PO_4$. The Tauc's equation is presented as below.

$$\alpha h\nu = A(h\nu - E_g)^{n/2}$$

Where α is the absorption coeffient, A is a constant and n depends on whether the transition semiconductor is indirect (n=4) or direct (n=1). Accordingly, the plot of $(\alpha h\nu)^{1/2}$versus hν as a function of photon energy has been displayed in Figure (b), (c) and (d).The band gap energy can be calculated by extrapolating the linear absorption edge of the curve. The $E_g$ of $Ag_3PO_4$, CuO and $Ag_3PO_4$/CuO microcrystal was found to be 2.36, 1.22 and 1.08 eV respectively. When the band gap decreased the transition, energy showed an obvious red shift. These results indicated that modified $Ag_3PO_4$/CuO could be narrow band gap of photocatalyst, which might be beneficial to improving the photocatalytic activity of the composites.

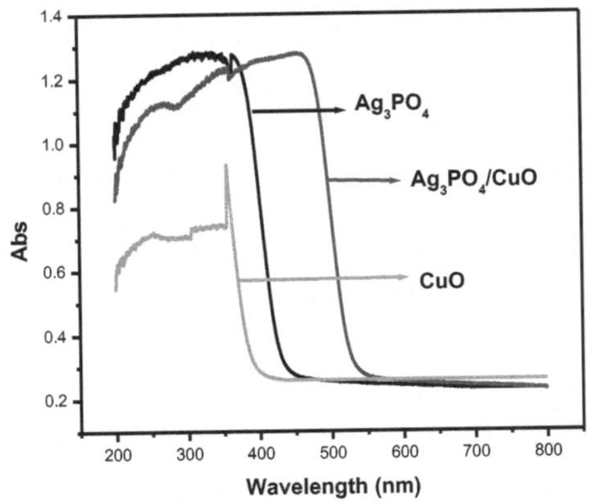


(a) UV-Vis- DRS spectrum of CuO, $Ag_3PO4$, $Ag_3PO4$/CuO

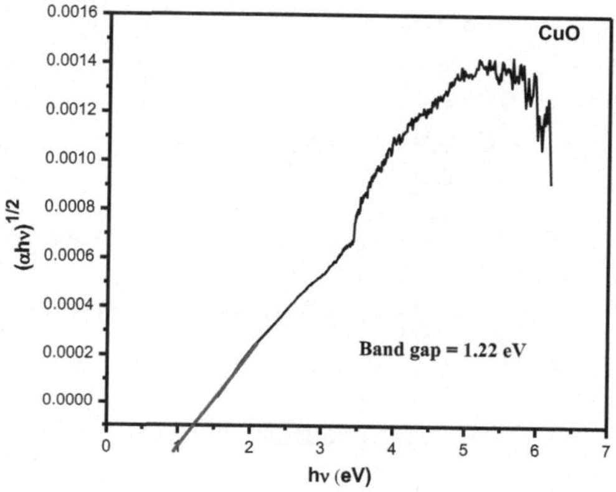


(b) Tauc plot of CuO

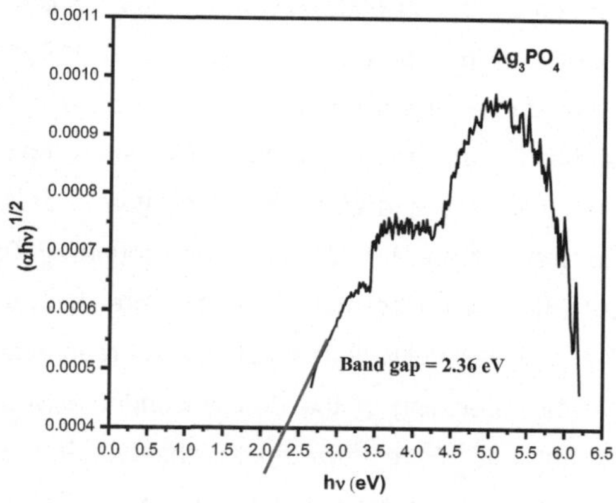


(c) Tauc plot of $Ag_3PO_4$

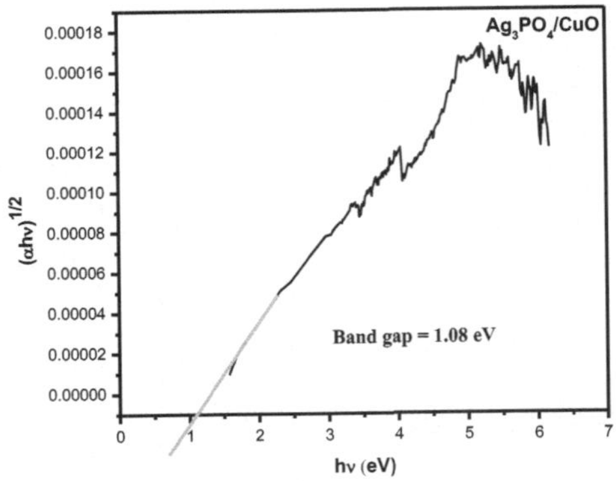


(d) Tauc plot of $CuO/Ag_3PO_4$

***FT-IR***

To certify the existence of interaction between CuO and $Ag_3PO_4$ nanoparticles FT-IR spectra of CuO, the pure $Ag_3PO_4$ and $Ag_3PO_4/CuO$ were examined as compared in Figure. The FT-IR spectrum shows bands at around 666, 417 and 471$cm^{-1}$,which can be assigned to the vibrations of Cu(II)-O bonds. There is sharp peak observed at 417$cm^{-1}$ in the spectrum CuO nanoparticles which is the characteristics of Cu-O bond formation. The broad absorption peak at around 3336$cm^{-1}$ is caused by the adsorbed water molecules since the nanocrystalline materials exhibit a high surface to volume ratio and thus absorb moisture. For the pure $Ag_3PO_4$ and the $Ag_3PO_4/CuO$ composites, a strong and broad absorption around 3200$cm^{-1}$ and sharp band at 1661$cm^{-1}$ were observed, which could be attribute to the stretching vibration of O-H and the bending vibration of H-O-H of water molecule respectively. A broad absorption band centered at 1419$cm^{-1}$ originated from the stretching of the doubly bonded oxygen vibration (P=O). Two absorption bands at 1023$cm^{-1}$ and 541$cm^{-1}$ were also observed in the spectra, and these two bands could be assigned to molecular vibrations of the phosphate ($PO_4^{3-}$).

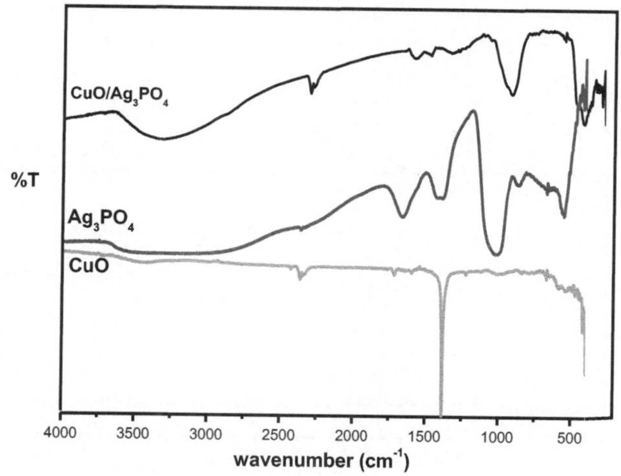


FT-IR spectrum of CuO, $Ag_3PO_4$ and $Ag_3PO_4$/CuO

### *XRD*

Figure the shows XRD patterns of the as-prepared samples. It is observed that CuO has monoclinic structure (JCPDS no: 48-1548) while $Ag_3PO_4$ has cubic primitive phase (JCPDS no: 89-7399). In addition, the $Ag_3PO_4$/CuO hybrid nanoparticles exhibited a coexistence of both CuO and $Ag_3PO_4$ phase. The diffraction pattern of CuO shows peak at 35.38˚, 38.6°, 48.66˚ and 53.33° which is correspond to ($\bar{1}$11), (111), (202) and (020) planes respectively. There after four sharp peaks at 29.7°, 33.4°, 36.6° and 42.5° which were good agreement with the diffraction form from the 200, 210, 211 and 220 crystal plane of a body centered cubic $Ag_3PO_4$ respectively. After CuO impregnation, the result sample of $Ag_3PO_4$/CuO with $Ag^+$ loading peak is at 25.9°, 29.7°, 31.9°, 32.3° , 33.0° and 36.6° which suggested that the prepared final product is perfect crystalline $Ag_3PO_4$ (29.7°, 33.0°, 36.6°) on the CuO support. As the $Ag^+$ loading increases, the peaks of as prepared composite photocatalyst of $Ag_3PO_4$/CuO at 38.7°, 58.7° 63.5°, were significantly sharper due to the larger $Ag_3PO_4$ content formed in the $Ag_3PO_4$/CuO.

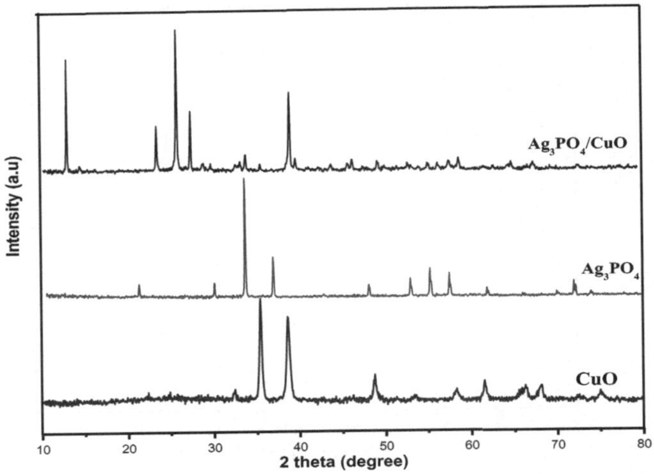


XRD pattern of CuO, $Ag_3PO_4$, $Ag_3PO_4/CuO$

***SEM, TEM and EDX***

The morphology of the nanocomposites was examined by SEM, and the micrographs are displayed in Figure (a), (b) and (c). All the nanocomposites are spherical like in shape and slightly agglomerated, favoring good photocatalytic activity. The TEM measurement was also performed in order to get detailed information about the morphology of the photocatalyst. TEM image of $Ag_3PO_4/CuO$ is shown in Figure (d). The prepared nanoparticles are spherical like shape, which is good agreement with the SEM results.

The existence of the metals on the surface of CuO was detected by EDX shown in Figure (e), (f) and (g) The EDX data of the nanocomposites are given in Table. The results revealed that all the elements (Ag, Cu, P, O) are clearly observed at their corresponding keV values.

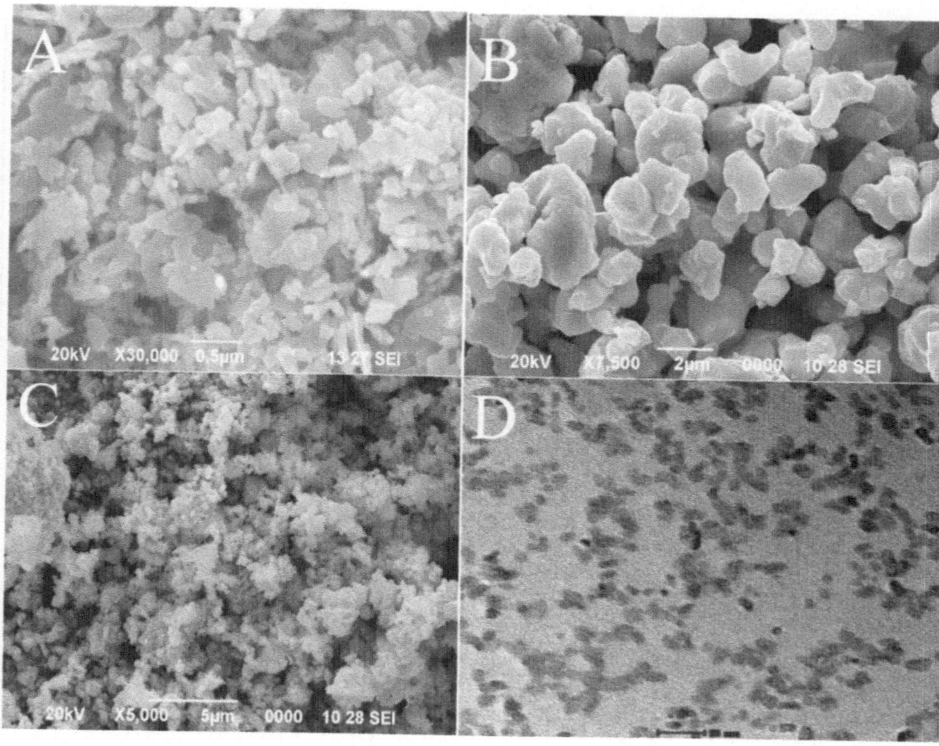


SEM and TEM images of $Ag_3PO_4/CuO$ NPs

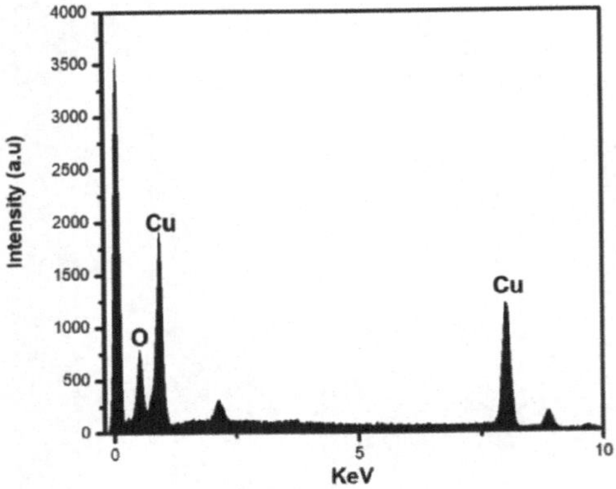


EDX spectrum of CuO

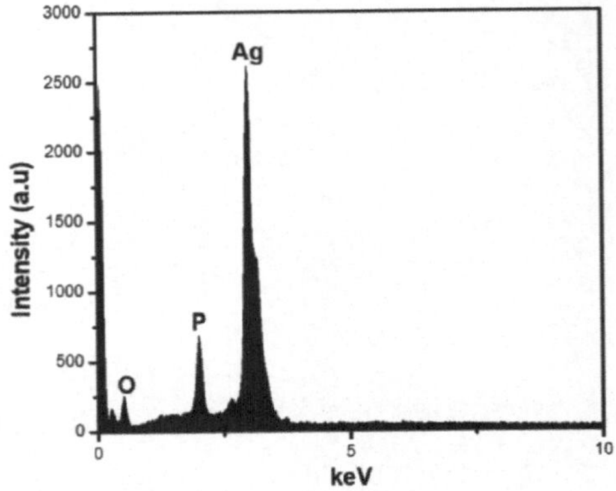


EDX spectrum of $Ag_3PO_4$

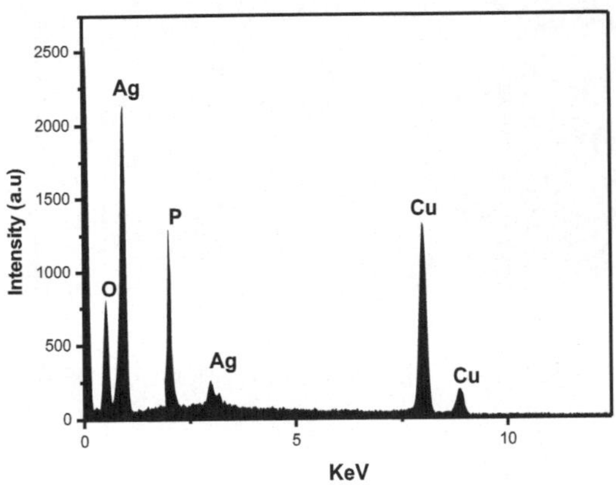


EDX spectrum of $Ag_3PO_4/CuO$

***EDX data of CuO, $Ag_3PO_4$ and $Ag_3PO_4$/CuO***

| S.No | Samples | Weight % | Atomic % | KeV |
|---|---|---|---|---|
| 1 | CuO | Cu = 78.49<br>O = 21.51 | Cu = 52.12<br>O = 47.88 | Cu = 2.14 eV<br>O = 9.68 eV |
| 2 | $Ag_3PO_4$ | O=21.01<br>P=6.71<br>Ag=72.27 | O=59.70<br>P=9.85<br>Ag=30.45 | O = 0.53<br>P = 2.139<br>Ag = 2.806 |
| 3 | $Ag_3PO_4$/CuO | O=25.30<br>Cu=63.85<br>Ag=4.85<br>P=6.71 | O=58.02<br>Cu=30.48<br>Ag=1.65<br>P=9.85 | O=2.02<br>Cu=15.090<br>Ag=3.151<br>P=2.139 |

***Photocatalytic activity of samples***

The photocatalytic test indicated that $Ag_3PO_4$/CuO composite samples showed good photocatalytic activities on degradation of the amaranth solution under visible light irradiation. The photodegradation process of amaranth was recorded by the UV-visible spectrum and all of the samples processed in the similar procedure. The UV-visible spectral changes of amaranth solution photode-gradation process over $Ag_3PO_4$/CuO composite sample are shown in Figure (a). During the photodegradation process of amaranth dye solution under the visible light irradiation, the pink color of the starting amaranth solution almost faded completely with the exposure time of about 180 min in the presence of $Ag_3PO_4$/CuO. In the degradation process, the absorption peaks at 520 nm corresponding to amaranth gradually decreases with extending the exposure time.

The photocatalytic degradation of amaranth over the CuO, $Ag_3PO_4$ and $Ag_3PO_4$/CuO composites prepared is shown in Figure (b). It indicated that the $Ag_3PO_4$/CuO composites showed the excellent photocatalytic activity, which may be ascribed to the improvement in charge transmission between the semiconductors CuO and $Ag_3PO_4$prolonged the charge carriers' lifetime. Moreover, the photocatalytic performance of the coupled semiconductors was also related to the surface contact between particles.

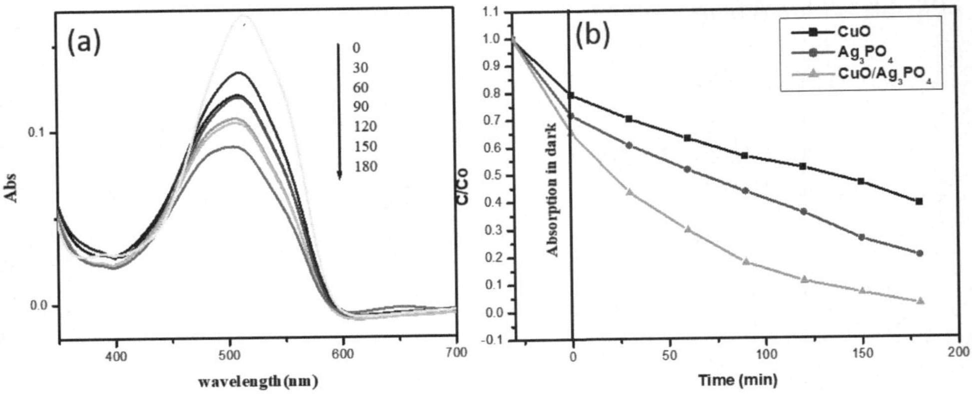


(a) The time dependent UV-Visible spectral change of Amaranth using $Ag_3PO_4/CuO$ under visible light irradiation

(b) Photodegradation of amaranth in the presence of CuO, $Ag_3PO_4$ and $Ag_3PO_4/CuO$

***Effect of initial dye concentration***

Figure shows the plot of decomposition vs time with respect to different initial concentration of the dye. It shows a high efficiency at 10μM initial concentration of the dye, which is due to the adsorption of the same. As the initial concentration of the dye increases, the degradation efficiency reduces. The possible reason is that, as the initial concentration of the dye increased, more dye molecule are adsorbed onto the surface of $Ag_3PO_4/CuO$. But, the adsorbed dye molecule are not degraded immediately because the intensity of the light and the catalyst amount is constant and also the light penetration is less. Also, with an increases in the dye concentration, the solution becomes more intense colored and the path length of the photons entering the solution is decreased thereby fewer photons reached the catalyst surface the catalyst surface. Hence, the productions of hydroxyl and superoxide radicals are limited or reduced. Therefore, Dye concentration also affects the efficiency of color removal. Initial concentration provides an important driving force to overcome all mass transfer resistances of the dye between the aqueous and solid phases. Hence, a higher initial concentration of dye may enhance the process.

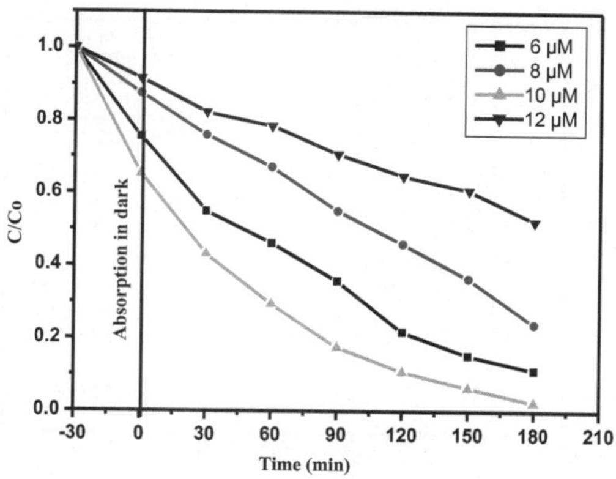


Effect of initial Amaranth concentration

***Effect of catalyst dose***

Experiments were carried out taking different amounts of $Ag_3PO_4/CuO$ keeping the dye concentration constant (10μM), in order to obtain an optimum condition with respect to the amount of catalyst used at which the photodegradation efficiency is maximum that can save unnecessary use of excess of photo-catalyst quantity-wise. Figure illustrates the effect of different amounts (0.075g/L to 0.15g/L) of $Ag_3PO_4/CuO$ on the decomposition of the dye molecules. It is observed that the efficiency increases up to 0.125g/L of the dye, beyond which it shows a gradual reduction in the rate constant. An increase in the efficiency is due to an increase in the number of active sites on $Ag_3PO_4/CuO$ available for the reaction, which in turn increases the rate of radical formation. The reduction in the rate constant may be due to the reduction in the penetration of light with surplus amount of CuO. The surplus addition of the catalyst makes the solution more turbid and light penetration is retarded. The addition of surplus catalyst also results in the deactivation of activated molecules by collision with ground state molecules. 0.125g/L of the catalyst dosage was found to be the optimum condition for treatment, which shows efficient photodegradation of Amaranth dye.

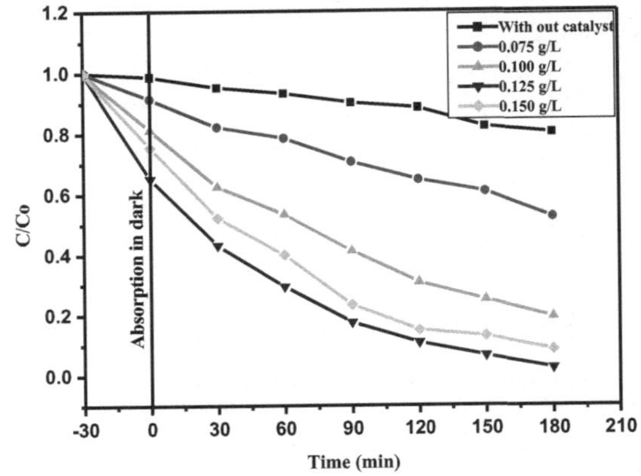


Effect of catalytic dosage

***Effect of initial pH***

Generally, the pH of the solution is an important parameter in the photocatalytic processes, since it not only plays an important role in the characteristics of dye, but also determines the surface charge properties of $Ag_3PO_4/CuO$, the size of aggregates formed the charge of dye molecules, adsorption of dye onto $Ag_3PO_4/CuO$ surface and the concentration of hydroxyl radicals. Hence, the photodecolorization of amaranth using $Ag_3PO_4/CuO$ was studied in pH range 2-6 and the results are shown in Figure. It was found that increase of solution pH from 2 to 4 increased the decolorization efficiency.

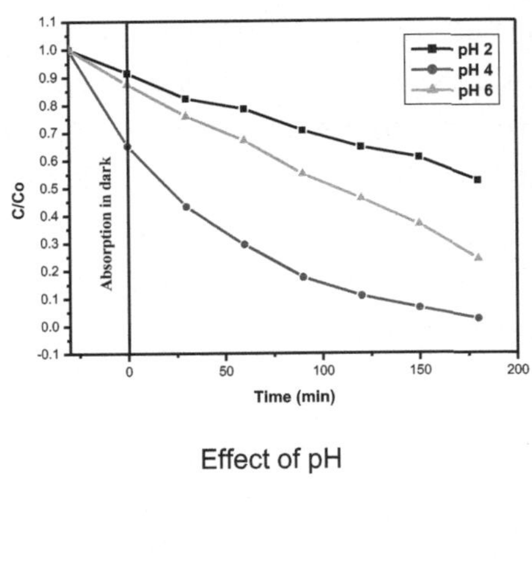


Effect of pH

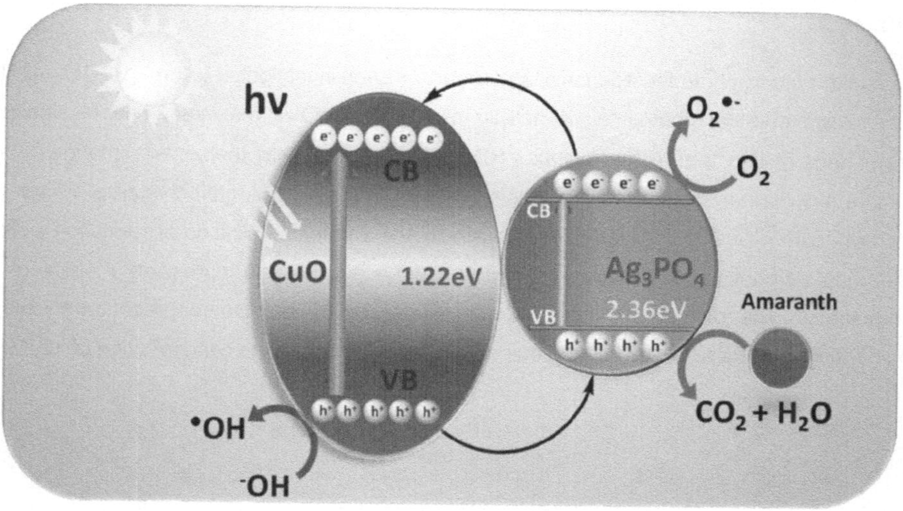


Photocatalytic mechanism of $Ag_3PO_4/CuO$

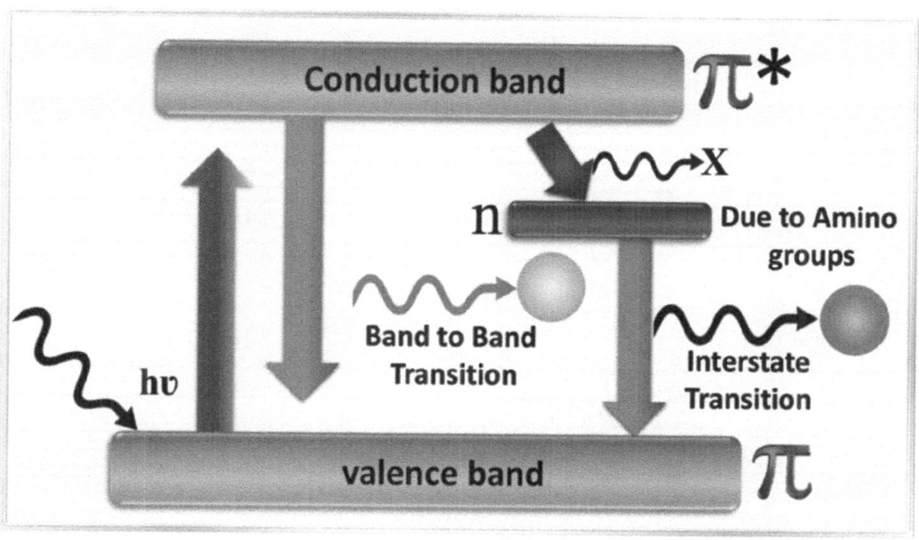


Photocatalysis mechanism of $Ag_3PO_4/CuO$ semiconductors

***Conclusion***

In this study, photodegradation of amaranth has been investigated using $Ag_3PO_4/CuO$. This study shows that the photocatalytic activity of $Ag_3PO_4/CuO$ is maximum due to significant absorption shift into the visible region. XRD results showed that there were changes in the structure of the catalyst as a result of doping with the metal ions. A nanocrystalline visible light sensitive $Ag_3PO_4/CuO$ is successfully synthesized by a simple chemical co-precipitation method. The enhanced photocatalytic activity of $Ag_3PO_4/CuO$ is due to the suppression of electron-hole recombination. The reaction conditions are optimized and maximum photodegradation is achieved within 180 min with a $Ag_3PO_4/CuO$ dosage of 0.125g/L and amaranth concentration of 10μM.

# Chapter-5

## Comparative Studies on the Synthesis of Copper Oxide Nano-Structures


### *Summary*

Synthesis of nanostructures for industrial usage is a challenge issue since most of the scale up production is not economically suitable. Here we have described two efficient synthesis approaches for copper (II) oxide nanostructures. In addition, we have compared the methods with current published procedures in terms of time and its impact to the environments. Our simple and environmentally friendly synthesis procedures can produce various Cu (II) oxide nano-structures. We have successfully synthesis $Cu(OH)_2$, CuO nanowire and CuO nano-particles. Moreover, they were characterized by Fourier transform infrared spectroscopy (FTIR), X-ray diffraction spectroscopy (XRD), Field emission scanning electron microscopy (FE-SEM), We have also explored the potential of these nanostructure for future development on biomedical applications.


### *Introduction*

The nanostructures of transition metal oxides have stimulated intensive research activities due to their exceptional properties arising from their high surface area/volume ratio and nanoscale quantum confinement effects. The transition metals oxides are an important class of semiconductors, which have applications in magnetic storage media, solar energy transformation, electronics and catalysis. Among the transition metal oxide group CuO, categorized into a p-type semiconductor with narrow and indirect energy band-gap of 1.2-1.8eV, and belongs to the monoclinic structure. The unique properties of physical, chemical and biological properties of CuO is broadly used in wide range of applications, such as superconductivity, photovoltaic properties, relatively stable, low cost and the antimicrobial activity. CuO is also a promising

Candidate due to its abundance, affordable price, chemical stability, and nontoxic nature. There are numerous strategies have been used for the developing synthesis of CuO nanostructures with different morphologies. Such as the sonochemical method, sol-gel technique, one-step solid-state reaction method at room temperature, electrochemical method, thermal decomposition of precursors, and co-implantation of metal and oxygen ions, and so on. Among these, solution-phase synthesis at room temperature is considered to be one of the most promising because of its high efficiency, low cost and potential high quality upscale production. These nanostructures are very stable, and their activity is longer when compared with organic anti-microbial agents.

Synthesis of CuO nanostructures is less expensive when compared to gold and silver nanoparticles which possess excellent antimicrobial agent because of their unusual crystal. Recent researchers have focused on green routes for the synthesis and production of nanoparticles.

In this study, the different morphologies of copper oxide nanostructures (CuO) were successfully synthesized by solution-phase synthesis in alkaline medium at room temperature. The effects of growth time on their morphology and crystallinity were investigated by Field Emission Scanning Electron Microscopy (FESEM), X-Ray Diffraction (XRD), and Fourier Transform Infrared Spectroscopic techniques.

## *Experimental and techniques*

### *Chemicals and Instrumentation*

Chemicals (copper sulfate ($CuSO_4.5H_2O$), sodium hydroxide (NaOH), were purchased from Sigma-Aldrich. All chemicals were used as received. Doubly distilled water is obtained from the laboratory. The as-synthesized nanostructures was well characterized with highly skilled technicians using Fourier transform infrared spectroscopy FTIR, X-ray diffraction pattern (PAN analytical, Northlands), and, field emission scanning electron microscopy (FE-SEM JSM-7610F).

## Methods for the Synthesis of CuO Nanostructures

### *Chemical Precipitation Method-I*

To synthesize $Cu(OH)_2$-nanoflakes via chemical precipitation method, a standard procedure was followed. About, 2.0g (0.25M) of $CuSO_4.5H_2O$ was dissolved in 50mL of purified water and 2.0g (1.0M) of sodium hydroxide is dissolved into 50ml of purified water individually. Then, the solutions were taken into RB flask and subject to under the magnetic stirring at 400 rpm for 2hrs. Meanwhile, NaOH solution was added drop by drop with continuous stirring. Finally, the prepared solution was allowed to sedimentation for 24hrs. The obtained precipitates were washed up to 3 times with purified water and ethanol under centrifugation at 4000rpm for 30 mints. Then, the collected precipitates were dried at 50$^{o}$C in a hot air oven for 2hrs.

***Chemical Precipitation method-II***

In this experiment the usual procedure was used, where 0.25M (4.0g) of $CuSO_4.5H_2O$ was dissolved in 100mL of purified water and 4.0g (1.0M) of sodium hydroxide is dissolved into 100ml of purified water individually. Then, the solutions were taken into RB flask and allowed to the magnetic stirring at 400rpm for 2hrs. Meanwhile, NaOH solution was added drop by drop under the vigorous stirring. During the reaction black color precipitate was formed. Finally, the prepared product was allowed to sedimentation for 10 hrs. The obtained precipitates were washed thrice with purified water and ethanol under centrifugation at 4000rpm for 30min. Then, the collected precipitates were dried at 60°C in a hot air oven for 4hrs. Then, the synthesized product was calcined at 400°C for 2hrs.

***Sonochemical Method***

The use of ultrasonic energy for the synthesis of CuO nanostructures that follows three steps: (1) formation (2) development, and (3) implosive collapse of the obtained micro cavities. In this method, reagent grade $CuSO_4.5H_2O$ was used as the Copper source to prepare the nanostructures and Sodium hydroxide used as a precipitating agent. In a typical synthesis, 0.2M of (3.19g) $CuSO_4.5H_2O$ and 0.8M of (3.19g) NaOH was dissolved into the 100ml of distilled water individually. Then alkali solution is taken in a burette and slowly added into the copper sulfate solution under the ultrasonication. This process continued for 3hrs in a cold condition. After the complete of reaction brown color precipitates was formed. Then the precipitates were centrifuged, washed with water and ethanol (95%) in a sequence and dried in an oven for 8hrs at 60-65°C. finally, the product was calcined at 400°C for 2hrs. All the experiments were carried out under the room temperature. The synthesis method is important for the properties of the final nanostructures, since it may control the size and morphology of the nanoparticles. In addition, these nanoparticles present various optical and magnetic properties, mechanical strengths and electrical resistivity, which differ from the characteristics of bulk solid material. Several methods for the synthesis of different CuO nanostructures have been used, and the most relevant approaches, along with the typical resulting particle sizes, are listed in Table 1.

**Table 1.** The synthesized CuO nanostructures with different methods are detailed below.

| S.No | | Synthesis methods | Shape of the products | Reaction time |
|---|---|---|---|---|
| 1. | $Cu(OH)_2$ | Chemical precipitation method | Nanoflakes | 2 hrs. room temperature |
| 2. | CuO | Chemical precipitation method | Nanowires | 2 hrs. room temperature |
| 3. | Cu(II)O | Sonochemical method | Sponge like NPs | 3 hrs. room temperature |

***Characterization of CuO Nanostructures***

The crystallinity and phase purity of CuO structures were characterized by XRD and the average crystalline size of the powders were calculated by Debye-Scherer formula. Figure. 1(A) shows the XRD patterns of $Cu(OH)_2$ complex obtained after drying the precipitate at 50°C. The diffraction peaks at 32.46°, 35.51°, 38.72°, 44.75°, 48.79°, 53.44°, and 58.29° can be indexed to the (110), ($\bar{1}$11), (022), (111), (150), (020), and ($\bar{1}$11), planes of orthorhombic $Cu(OH)_2$, respectively matching the data (JCPDS 80-0656), and also the XRD patterns of CuO NWs annealed to a temperature of 400°C. The peaks in the XRD patterns of CuO NWs were compared with the standard data. Fig. 1(B) shows the major peaks at 2θ values at 32.75°, 35.55°, 38.85°, 48.75°, 53.85°, 58.35°, 61.55°, 66.45°, 68.15°, 72.45°, and 74.85° are indexed to the (110), ($\bar{1}$11), (111), ($\bar{2}$02), (020), ($\bar{1}$13), ($\bar{3}$11), (220), (311), and (004) planes, respectively. These XRD patterns attribute to the monoclinic CuO NWs crystal which has good agreement with the standard JCPDS data (ref no.5-0661) and there are no any other characteristic peaks of impurities such as $Cu(OH)_2$, $Cu_2O$, or precursors were observed, indicating the formation of a pure phase CuO NWs. Fig. 1(C) depicts the peaks at the formation of Cu(II)O NPs. All the diffractions were well matched with the monoclinic phase of Cu(II)O (standard JCPDS File No: 048-1548). Diffraction peaks with 2θ 35.45°, 38.81°, 48.77° and 61.47° respectively indexed to the (002), (111), (020) and (022) reflection planes.

The average crystalline size of the all CuO nanostructures was examined by the full-width half maximum value of prominent diffraction peak of the XRD pattern using Scherer's equation as follows,

$$X_s = k\lambda / \beta \cos\theta \rightarrow (3)$$

Where, Xs is the size of crystalline, $\lambda$ is X-ray wavelength, ß is FWHM (full width at half maximum) of the diffraction peak, θ is diffraction angle and k is Scherer's constant. The crystalline size was calculated for the diffraction planes and the average size of each nanostructure to be 14.89nm $Cu(OH)_2$, 10.17nm CuO NWs and 10.66nm Cu(II)O respectively. The experimental results also found similar to the reported diffraction patterns of CuO structures.

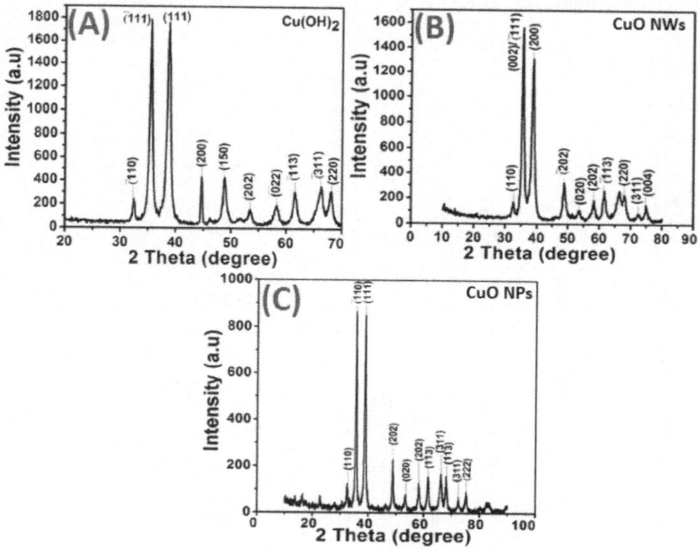


Fig. 1. (A) X-ray diffraction patterns of as-prepared $Cu(OH)_2$ CuO NWs (B) and CuO NPs (C).

In order to understand the chemical and structural nature of the synthesized $Cu(OH)_2$ and CuO NWs the effect of the chemicals used in the FTIR analysis was carried out. Fig.2(A) represents the FTIR spectrum recorded for the $Cu(OH)_2$ and CuO NWs in the range of 400 to 4,000cm$^{-1}$. In the as synthesized $Cu(OH)_2$, presence of peak at 3433.71cm$^{-1}$ reflects stretching mode of hydroxyl groups in the $Cu(OH)_2$. The peak at 1661.02cm-1 reflects the bending mode of the absorbed water in the as synthesized $Cu(OH)_2$. In the FTIR spectrum, CuO NWs peaks at

497.48cm$^{-1}$ and 1117.53cm$^{-1}$ corresponds to strong Cu-O stretching vibrations. The peak at 1641.79 corresponds to C=O stretching acidic groups. Bands at 3433.96 cm$^{-1}$ may be attributed to the Cu–OH groups shown in the Fig.2 (B). Normally, CuO vibrations are observed at wavenumbers less than 600cm$^{-1}$.

In the FTIR spectrum of CuO Fig. 2(C), peak at 501.71cm$^{-1}$ and 1112.38cm$^{-1}$ corresponds to strong Cu-O stretching vibrations. The peak at 1628.74 corresponds to C=O stretching vibrational groups and the peaks at 2357.71 corresponds to the O-H broad stretching vibrations. Bands at 3417.71 cm$^{-1}$ may be attributed to the Cu–OH groups. All the peaks of the vibrational spectra that confirms the defined CuO nanostructures.

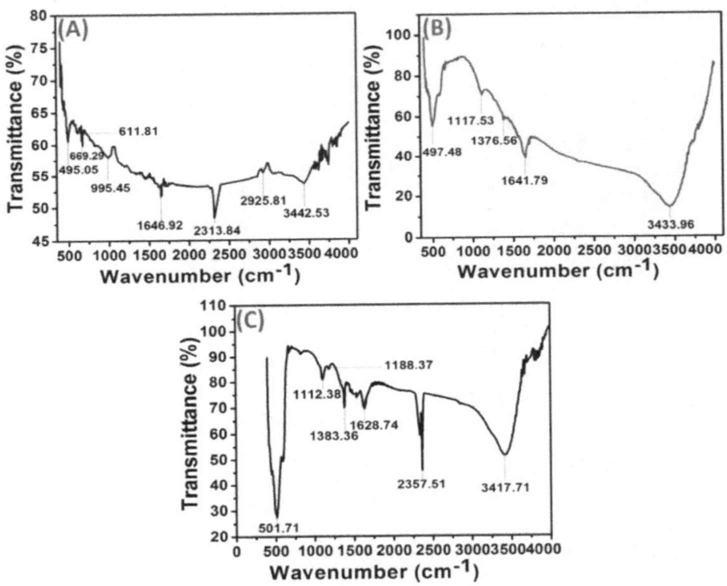


Fig. 2. (A) FTIR spectrum of $Cu(OH)_2$ CuO NWs (B) and CuO NPs (C)

The surface morphology of CuO nanostructures were confirmed by FESEM images with different magnification (Fig. 3). Fig. 3(A) displays the FE-SEM image at a low-magnification (X 15,000) of $Cu(OH)_2$. The newly synthesized CuO NWs consists mainly uniformly and aggregated bundle of wires like structure in huge quantities with an individual size ranging from 0.6 to 1.0μm. The high magnification (X65,000) FE-SEM image of CuO NWs Fig. 3(B) displays the bundle consisted of huge number of nanowires and displays the active sites of CuO NWs. Fig. 3 (C) reveals the morphology of CuO NPs with the magnification of (X30,000). All the synthesized nanostructures are compared in the table 1.

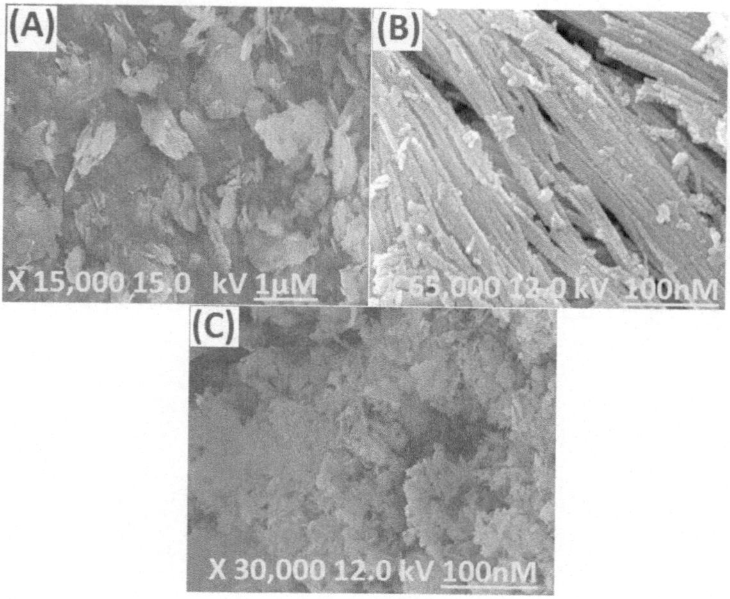


Fig. 3. FE-SEM of as-synthesized $Cu(OH)_2$ (A) CuO NWs (B) and CuO NPs (C)

***Conclusion***

In this study, we successfully synthesized the different CuO nanostructures by green chemical methods and their confirmed by XRD, FTIR and FE-SEM analysis. The average crystalline and particle size of the nanostructures are detailed. As the synthesized nanostructures are applied for the future biomedical applications. This nanostructure is environmental friendly.

**Note**:

*The book is published for understanding and academic purpose only, for new research students. The author of this book declares that, there is no conflict of interest and he is the responsible.*

*Palpandi. K*

*Quality control data analyst*

*National human rights security of bureau (Social service), Reg.NO:IV-07/2024*

*Tamilnadu state, Coimbatore district,*

*India.*